The Pathways to Peace

Anger Management Workbook

Anger is a major contributor to society and family ills. This book is non-shaming, non-blaming, and comprehensive in its focus. It will be life-giving to the reader who is looking for answers to problems in anger. A significant contribution to the field of mental health.

— Claudia A. Black, MSW, Ph.D., author of
It Will Never Happen to Me

It would be hard to imagine a more timely work than *The Pathways to Peace* workbook by William Fleeman. I especially find Mr. Fleeman's use of worksheets helpful. It is one thing to read a truth. It is quite another to integrate that truth into one's life so there is concrete change. Would that everyone in this violent, angry time would read and use *Pathways to Peace*.

— Earnie Larsen, author of *Anger to Forgiveness*

The Pathways to Peace Anger Management Workbook and program saved me from relapsing back into alcoholism after the 9/11 attacks on New York City. The workbook helped me overcome a major block—anger and rage. It saved my recovery.

— Ken Q., New York City Fireman

DEDICATION

*This book is dedicated to the hundreds of Pathways to Peace members
who have contributed so much to this new, revised edition of the workbook,
and to the continuing growth of the Pathways to Peace movement.*

*With loving appreciation to my wife, Jan, for her support,
and for the unconditional love that I must work so hard to
express but that is her natural gift.*

*With special thanks to George Domby, my good friend and colleague,
for his sensitive and exquisite editorial work.*

Ordering

Trade bookstores in the U.S. and Canada please contact:

Publishers Group West
1700 Fourth Street, Berkeley CA 94710
Phone: (800) 788-3123   Fax: (800) 351-5073

Hunter House books are available at bulk discounts for textbook course adoptions; to qualifying community, health-care, and government organizations; and for special promotions and fund-raising. For details please contact:

Special Sales Department
Hunter House Inc., PO Box 2914, Alameda CA 94501-0914
Phone: (510) 865-5282   Fax: (510) 865-4295
E-mail: ordering@hunterhouse.com

Individuals can order our books from most bookstores, by calling **(800) 266-5592**, or from our website at **www.hunterhouse.com**

The Pathways to Peace

Anger Management
Workbook

William Fleeman
Director and Founder
of *Pathways to Peace*

Hunter House PUBLISHERS

Hunter House Inc., Publishers
PO Box 2914
Alameda CA 94501-0914

This is a revised edition of *Pathways to Peace: The Program on Anger Management and Violence Prevention* first published in 2000 by Transformations Enterprises.

Library of Congress Cataloging-in-Publication Data

Fleeman, William.
    The pathways to peace anger management workbook / William Fleeman.
        p. cm.
    ISBN-13: 978-0-89793-418-3 (sp.) — ISBN-13: 978-0-89793-417-6 (pbk.)
    ISBN-10: 0-89793-418-0 (sp.) — ISBN-10: 0-89793-417-2 (pbk.)
    1. Anger. 2. Violence—Psychological aspects. I. Title.
BF575.A5 F58 2003
152.4'7—dc21   2002152620

Project Credits

Cover Design: Brian Dittmar Graphic Design
Book Design: Hunter House
Book Production: Jinni Fontana
Copy Editor: Rachel E. Bernstein
Proofreader: John David Marion
Acquisitions Editor: Jeanne Brondino
Editor: Alexandra Mummery
Publicity Coordinators: Earlita K. Chenault, Lisa E. Lee
Sales & Marketing Coordinator: Jo Anne Retzlaff
Customer Service Manager: Christina Sverdrup
Order Fulfillment: Lakdhon Lama
Administrator: Theresa Nelson
Computer Support: Peter Eichelberger
Publisher: Kiran S. Rana

Printed and Bound by Sheridan Books, Ann Arbor, Michigan

Manufactured in the United States of America

9 8 7 6 5   Third Edition   09 10 11 12 13

Contents

Introduction

Pathways to Peace, Inc., is a self-help anger management and violence prevention program. *The Pathways to Peace Anger Management Workbook* is the official guide for Pathways to Peace groups.

The Pathways to Peace Anger Management Workbook is an interactive guide to help you understand, and then change, your angry behavior. The lessons and exercises in the workbook follow a logical sequence, which is especially useful in situations where structured learning is desirable. The readability level of *The Pathways to Peace Anger Management Workbook* makes the material accessible to most people.

This workbook can be used by individuals as a hands-on learning tool or by agencies, institutions, and schools as a textbook/workbook for anger management and violence prevention programs. *The Pathways to Peace Anger Management Workbook* can also be used by Pathways to Peace groups as a more structured approach to learning how to manage anger and rage.

This workbook includes writing exercises to help you look at your own experiences and your anger. These exercises are not a test; they don't have right or wrong answers. They are to help you understand yourself. You write the answers down, instead of just thinking about them, so that you can look back at your answers and remember them. Write your answers in this workbook or write them in a special notebook or journal. Wherever you write them down, keep the answers all together, because some exercises later in the workbook require you to look back at your answers from earlier exercises.

It's always OK to reread a section or a lesson while you're answering the exercises. Remember it's not a test. The important thing is that you understand every lesson well, and you understand how it applies to your life. Feel free to reread any section until you understand it.

How Long Will It Take to Complete the Workbook?

The workbook is designed to be completed in sixteen to eighteen weeks, with a minimum of one hour of study per week. The actual completion time will depend on how much time you spend reading the material and completing the exercises. A program of almost any length could be designed; for example, a program plan could be designed with a completion target of one year or more.

How Long Will It Take to Heal from Anger and Rage?

This workbook is only a beginning. Healing from anger and rage takes longer than a few months, since healing requires more than a change in behavior. Changing angry behavior is the easy part, while changing at the character level takes much longer and is much harder. True healing does not occur until the character has been transformed.

Full recovery from a long-standing pattern of anger and rage takes a minimum of two to three years. *Maintaining recovery is an ongoing, lifelong process.* Work hard, have patience, and be forgiving of yourself.

The Problem

All over the world thousands of people are verbally abused, physically assaulted, maimed, or murdered every day because of anger and rage. Families are ruined, marriages ended, children traumatized, careers lost, opportunities missed, and personal and public property destroyed. *This* is the problem.

Pathways to Peace: A Solution

Pathways to Peace offers a solution to the problem. The Pathways to Peace program and workbook do not focus on fixing the social injustices that contribute to the problem. They do not focus on changing the myths that have created an international culture of violence. The solution to this enormous problem lies with the individuals who are caught up in angry and violent behavior. The Pathways to Peace program and workbook focus on helping angry people change and grow. When enough people change and grow, a *movement* is born. Pathways to Peace is a movement that can lead to change and growth around the world. By becoming part of Pathways to Peace, you can be part of the solution.

A Message to the Person Struggling to Change

Like many others, you may feel you are alone in your struggle—but you are not alone. You may feel that everyone has given up on you—but not everyone has given up. You may have suffered severe personal consequences because of your behavior, and you may feel so overwhelmed with guilt and shame that you have come to believe that no one could possibly care whether you live or die. But there are those who care.

Scattered throughout this workbook are brief stories just like yours, written by men and women just like you. These people have shared their personal histories with you to make it easier for you to understand and to relate to the material in the workbook. Writing down their stories was often painful to the writers, because it required them to recall things and events they would rather not think about. They struggled through the pain because they want to help you.

Like you, these men and women have struggled with anger and rage. Like you, they have felt alone and powerless. Like you, some have suffered severe personal consequences because of their behavior. Once filled with overwhelming guilt and shame they, too, felt that no one cared.

But the people who have shared their personal stories in this workbook haven't struggled in vain; they have struggled and won. Through the Pathways to Peace program, they found help for their problem. They found acceptance and support, and they learned skills to help them deal with anger triggers. They learned how to live in harmony with their families, their friends, their employers, and their coworkers. The people who wrote down their stories will tell you that the struggle wasn't easy, but they succeeded. They changed their behavior, stopped the violence once and for all, and are now reaping the rewards. They are living reasonably happy, productive lives. Most of these people continue to learn and to grow by participating in Pathways to Peace self-help groups in their community. These people care about you, because they understand. They sincerely hope that you find your *pathway to peace.*

PART ONE

Understand the Problem

1

The Self-Assessment Process

To "assess" means to take an honest look. To "self-assess" means to take an honest look at yourself. You must take an honest look at yourself as a person with an anger problem.

The author of *The Pathways to Peace Anger Management Workbook* sometimes uses the first person designation "I" and sometimes the third person "Bill." Using the first person helps him to connect and relate with the reader on a deeper, more personal level. It also aids him in the process of self-disclosure. The use of the third person, on the other hand, assists him in navigating the ideas and concepts covered in the text and helps him convey lessons to be learned in a more objective fashion.

LESSON 1 ~ Pathways to Peace Founder's Story

Pathways to Peace is a self-help program for people with anger problems. This workbook is the official guidebook for that program. William (Bill) Fleeman founded Pathways to Peace.

Bill used many tools to help him change his angry behavior. He did a self-assessment, and he wrote his story as part of his self-assessment.

In his story Bill tells about his childhood, revealing some of the things that happened to him. He explains how he developed his anger habit, and how his anger habit then turned into an addiction to anger. He talks about some of the violent things he did while angry, even confessing that he caused harm to others. He talks about his consequences. Then Bill tells about his recovery and about what his life is like now.

Bill's story may be different from yours—his specific experiences will probably be different from yours, but Bill's feelings were probably similar to yours. Don't fall into the trap of thinking your story is not so bad compared to Bill's, or that it is much worse. Focus on the *feelings* Bill talks about. That is the best way to compare your story to Bill's.

Bill's Story

Writing down my story was an important part of my recovery from my lifelong problem with anger. Writing my story helped me understand why I developed an anger habit and why my habit became a full-blown addiction to anger and rage. It helped motivate me to change.

Also it helped me find out how to change. Writing my story was an important part of my self-assessment.

My father was an angry, violent army drill sergeant from Indianapolis. He was also an alcoholic. He abandoned me and my mother when I was an infant. My mother was the daughter of a northern Michigan lumberjack. My grandfather had a problem with alcohol and a temper like a rhinoceros. After my father left, my mother took me to live with my maternal grandparents. We all lived in a small rented house near downtown. I had no brothers or sisters.

Later in my childhood, I tried to figure out why my father left. I decided it must have been my fault. I decided something must be wrong with me. I decided I was defective. I *felt* defective. I must be defective, I thought, or my father wouldn't have left.

Soon I developed the belief that you can't trust people to stick by you. If your own father leaves you, my child's mind reasoned, who can you trust? You can't trust anyone. Period. That is what I came to believe.

My mother often worked two jobs in order to support me and my grandparents. My grandmother kept house and took care of me. My grandfather worked part-time as a night dispatcher at a taxi cab company.

My grandfather was often violent when he drank. I saw violence in my home from an early age. My earliest memory of family violence happened when I was three or four. To this day I can remember it as though it happened only yesterday. That is the way the brain remembers trauma.

It was early one winter day. My grandfather had returned home from his dispatcher's job and was drunk. I stood at the front window and watched two other drunken men help my grandfather up the snowy walk to the door. My mother and grandmother were watching, too. Glancing up, I saw rage in my mother's eyes. My grandmother was angry, too. The two men left my grandfather at the door, and then staggered back to the car parked at the curb and drove away.

The door was locked. My grandfather pounded drunkenly on the door and waited in the cold for it to open. My mother waited until the other men were gone. Then she opened the door. My grandfather staggered inside. My mother slammed the door behind him. Screaming and cursing, she shoved my grandfather to the floor. She leaped in the air, then came down on his chest on her knees. Too drunk to defend himself, my grandfather lay passively on the floor while my mother pounded his face with her fists. My grandmother stood back crying and wringing her hands. I stood with my back pasted to the far wall of the room. I watched, terrified. I felt totally *powerless*.

I never felt safe after that experience. From that day on I felt as though something terrible could happen at any time, without warning. I felt afraid all of the time. That event left me with the belief that the world was a very dangerous place, and that you had to be on guard all of the time.

My feelings about my grandfather were a conflicting mixture of love and fear. He was a hard-drinking old lumberjack who loved whiskey and stud poker. It was hard for him to show tender feelings. Looking back, though, I believe he loved me in his way and did the best he could.

When I was five years old, my grandfather died. I felt a great loss. Although he had been abusive, he was the only "father" I had known. I plunged into a depression and withdrew into a silent inner world. My grandmother grew sick with grieving and ended up in the hospital. There was no money to hire a sitter to care for me, so my mother took me out of school and sent me to stay with an aunt. I felt totally abandoned and alone. Time and my aunt's loving kindness healed my depression, yet I would suffer bouts of depression most of the rest of my life.

I don't remember much about the year my grandfather died. But I do remember feeling that my grandfather's death was my fault. It left me with a growing sense of guilt. Of course, my feeling of guilt surrounding my grandfather's death was based on a faulty belief. I believed that when bad things happened, it was because I had done something terribly wrong. That was the way my child's mind understood my grandfather's death. As I grew older, I developed an overriding sense of guilt. There were times when I felt everything was my fault. Later that sense of guilt turned into feelings of anger and rage. I learned to use anger to mask depression and sadness. My brain would find anger and rage more pleasurable than guilt and depression.

When I was seven, my mother remarried. She married another soldier, Jim, who was a WWII combat veteran. Like thousands of others, he'd returned from the war traumatized and an alcoholic. My stepfather resented me at times. He naturally wished to have a son or daughter of his own, which never happened. But he was kind and treated me well, and he was not violent in the home.

My grandmother was religious. She made sure I went to Sunday school and church every Sunday. I did not like Sunday school. I felt self-conscious and out of place. I felt I didn't fit. The bleeding figure of Christ looking down from the cross scared me. Sometimes I thought I saw my grandfather's bloodied face there instead of Christ's. I carried deep and painful feelings of guilt and unworthiness into the church with me. I felt God would only abandon me anyway, as my earthly father had done by choice and my grandfather by death. When I was seven, I stopped going to church, and I stopped believing in God.

I got in my first fistfight when I was eight. It happened at school. It was a rainy day in early spring. A kid made fun of me because he knew I didn't have a father. From early childhood I had felt worthless and alone, powerless and afraid. That's how kids often feel when their father abandons them. Sometimes I told people my father had been killed in the war. But the kid who taunted me knew that was a lie because one of my cousins had told him the truth. The kid's remarks hooked my feelings of abandonment. What he said pushed my self-esteem even lower. I felt a sinking feeling in my stomach, and then I shoved the kid down the school steps.

Watching the kid tumble down the steps, I felt my first "anger high." The other kids who cheered me on added to the high. The high lasted only an instant, but for that instant I felt a sense of power I had never felt before. I felt confident instead of afraid, accepted instead of rejected, strong instead of weak. What I felt, felt good. Pleasurable. The kid was not hurt, and neither of us suffered bad results. The teacher who broke up the fight merely talked to us.

Later that day the high went away, and all of the negative feelings I felt about myself came back. But that fight on the school steps changed me and the change lasted most of the rest of my life. A new part had been added to my character, a part I could not seem to control, a part I was not even aware of, a part that would continue to seek the rush of power I felt when I shoved that kid down the stairs. Over time, that part would grow big and strong, until finally it would run my life. Later I would find out what it was. It was *anger and rage.* That fight on the school steps also caused me to form a new belief: *Anger is power.* That belief influenced my behavior for the next thirty-five years.

I moved with my mother, stepfather, and grandparents to Detroit, Michigan, when I was thirteen. We moved into a "tough" neighborhood called Washington Square, and I went to a "tough" school called South Side High. As usual, I felt out of place. Then I joined a street gang, the "Washington Square Gang." I had a lot in common with the other gang members. Their fathers had abandoned them, their grandmothers raised them while their mothers worked two jobs, and their grandfathers were alcoholics. Violence and alcoholism and drug abuse existed in their homes, and they were angry like me.

Most of the gang members went to South Side High. We hung out together in the hallways, protecting each other from real or imagined taunts from other students. For the first time in my life, I felt safe. For the first time in my life, I felt I belonged. But I didn't feel safe or accepted anyplace else, only in the gang. I got into fights in school and on the street as my anger got worse. I punched walls, bolted out of classrooms, and slammed doors. My peers applauded my behavior, and that made the consequences seem worthwhile.

I ran away from home at fourteen. I wanted to get as far away as possible from my family and from South Side High. I came back tired, but unchanged.

By the time I got to ninth grade, South Side High found my behavior unacceptable. And it was. The teachers and administrators had done their best—I had not. My behavior had gotten worse instead of better. The school expelled me at the beginning of the spring term when I was fifteen years old. My mother protested but it didn't help. There had been too many angry outbursts involving other students as well as teachers. Also, I was failing all subjects, which meant I would have to return to South Side in the fall and repeat ninth grade. The South Side staff did not want to deal with me for another whole year. Being expelled greatly increased my status in the street gang. For me, that was the payoff.

The following September, I got into very serious trouble because of my anger. I was arrested and placed in a detention center. I refused to reveal names of some others who were involved, so I was placed in solitary confinement to await my court date and sentencing. I was in solitary for thirty-six days, in a windowless 8' x 10' cell with a solid steel door, a cot, a sink, and a toilet. I spent my sixteenth birthday there.

After sentencing I was taken to a reformatory in Jackson, Michigan. At the reformatory a guard punched me in the spine for talking in line. He punched me so hard I literally saw stars. On another occasion a different guard slashed my lower back with a dog choker chain that he carried around as a key chain.

Because we were watched so closely, few fights broke out at the reformatory. But I had one fight there when another kid from Detroit made fun of me and I got embarrassed. The feeling of embarrassment is what triggered my anger. It was not much of a fight, and we didn't get caught and punished because the other kids covered for us.

Then I joined the reformatory boxing team and had some legal fights. I was a kid with an anger problem, and the coaching staff taught me how to be more effectively violent. (I have never been able to figure that out.) I also lifted weights.

After my release I was on parole until I was nineteen. I drank too much and got violent at parties. After I got off parole, I hit the road. I was restless and unhappy, and I still felt my life had no meaning. I hitchhiked to California, met a girl there, and got married. I was twenty.

I went to college for a short time in California. In those days in California, you could get into a community college even if you hadn't finished high school. If you were eighteen or over and could pass the entrance exam, by law they had to let you enroll. I had always been a reader and had read widely on many subjects. Before I had been expelled, I used to skip school every chance I got. I would hide from the truant officer at the public library and read a lot of books while sitting in the back between rows. I took the entrance exam at Los Angeles City College and passed. I was twenty years old, so they had to let me in.

Meanwhile, I was still using anger and rage to deal with the world, and my new wife was having a hard time dealing with my anger. Before I completed my second semester, she left me and went to San Francisco. The marriage lasted a year and we'd had no children. I dropped out of college.

I was drinking too much and I had developed a drug habit. Eventually, I became addicted to speed and downers. One night I got drunk on tequila and downers and the results were bad. While I was blacked out (but on my feet), I got into a fight with my best friend and tried to kill him. I woke up in the morning feeling bad and looking worse. My friend came over later to tell me the story. He said I had gone into a rage the previous night and tried to choke him in the front seat of his car. He said I'd also kicked out one side of the windshield of his car. At first I didn't believe him, but then he showed me the bruises and fingernail marks on his throat and he showed me the smashed windshield. He said he had managed to pry my hands loose. Then he'd slammed my face into the dashboard of the car and knocked me out. He said he was sorry he had hurt me. I felt deeply ashamed and could not face my friend again for several months.

I went back to Detroit at age twenty-three. I divorced my first wife, and then married again. I had a son. I worked in machine shops and learned some skills, but meanwhile, my anger got worse. I lost ten machine shop jobs over the next ten years because of my anger.

I got a DWI when I was thirty. Once again I was locked up, this time in the drunk tank. I felt humiliated and ashamed. The police said they would have allowed someone to come and take me home if I hadn't been so verbally abusive.

Finally I had to leave Detroit again because I had run out of machine shop owners who were willing to put up with my anger. The word had gotten around that I was a good worker but couldn't get along with people, especially people in authority, like machine shop owners and machine shop foremen. I moved my family to Indianapolis when I was thirty-three.

When I moved to Indianapolis, I rediscovered the sport of weight lifting. I quit my machine shop job and went to work as a health club instructor. I had a knack for selling memberships and a talent for helping out-of-shape people with low self-esteem get back into shape. The new job helped increase my own self-esteem, but my anger habit followed me into my new career. One night I got angry with one of the other instructors and picked a fight with him. I lost my job because of the fight. I got another health club job a week later and lost that one, too, when I got angry at the club Christmas party and got into a fight with the owner. I went back to work in machine shops.

I joined a power-lifting club, the Central Indiana Weight Lifting Club, and started to compete. My teammates urged me to stop drinking and using drugs, saying I could probably establish a new bench-press record if I stopped. I joined a twelve-step program and stopped drinking, and then nine months later I became a bench-press champion. I opened a health club—but lost it because of my anger. When I opened my club, I'd had no money for equipment, so some of my power-lifting friends had let me use their equipment in exchange for memberships. My angry outbursts at the gym soon drove them away. They took their equipment with them, so I had to close up shop.

I moved my family back to Detroit again. I stayed off booze and other drugs and went back to machine shop work. I became shop foreman, but then I had an anger outburst and got fired.

About nine months after I stopped drinking and using other drugs, I had an unusual experience—an awakening of some sort, a spiritual awakening. Actually, words cannot describe what happened. But the word "spiritual" comes close. It was like what happened to Scrooge in *A Christmas Carol* by Charles Dickens.

The experience made me aware that I did have a purpose for being alive, and what I had been doing with my life up to then was not it. That strange experience gave me hope, and some of the fear that had haunted me for so long went away. I felt a pressing need to find out what I was supposed to do with my life, and, whatever it was, I knew that anger and rage would not help me accomplish it. I wanted to stop the violence but did not know how.

The experience changed my outlook but not my behavior. It turned my face toward the light, but it did not take away my anger and rage. Because of my anger, my second marriage ended in divorce. I decided I was a loser in the marriage department, too, but later I married again. I brought my son with me into this new union, my third marriage. Soon after, my new wife became pregnant.

My anger was still a problem. I had an outburst of rage one night and my wife called the police. I didn't hurt her, but I scared her. At first, I felt guilty and ashamed, and then I plunged into a depression. Finally, I saw a counselor. When I admitted feeling suicidal, the counselor advised hospitalization for depression. I checked into a locked ward in Pontiac, Michigan, and stayed there forty-five days. While I was there, I discovered my purpose. I found out what my mission was, and the depression lifted.

My wife, who was then pregnant, went to New York while I was in the hospital. My first son and I joined her in New York soon after my second son was born.

I had discovered that my purpose was to help people. As a recovering alcoholic and drug addict, I was eligible for state and federal education funding as a part of my rehabilitation and was able to go to college to become a counselor. My last violent act occurred just before I started college. The person upstairs was playing his music too loud and keeping the baby awake. I told him to turn down the music, and when he refused, I kicked down his door. He called the police, who came to the building but didn't arrest me. By then my wife could stand no more, so she took my new son and ran away again. Afraid of how I might react if I was able to find her and my son, she took an assumed name and went into hiding.

I tried to find my son for nineteen years, but was unsuccessful. Finally when he was twenty years old, he found me, and we had a wonderful reunion. His mother and I met not long after and made amends to each other. My son and I are still in touch. If I hadn't overcome my addiction to anger, we probably never would have met.

When I finished my associate's degree, I became a counselor at a drug and alcohol clinic. One of my clients got drunk and had a standoff with the police, during which he shot at them with a .22 caliber rifle. The sheriff's department called and asked me to do a telephone intervention, but I was too late. He was too drunk. He even took two shots at me.

A sharpshooter from a SWAT team came from behind and killed my client. I went into a rage and verbally attacked the police. The director of the agency where I worked said my behavior was unprofessional and inappropriate, and he fired me. Anger had robbed me again. Of course I blamed the police for my client's death, but I blamed myself more. I plunged into a depression again.

At last I saw what the real problem was. At last I understood. I was *addicted* to anger the way I had been addicted to alcohol and other drugs! My anger was a primary addiction. And I saw I was not the only one, anger and rage was a serious problem for thousands of people. At last I knew *exactly* what my personal mission was. My mission was to help others like myself, and not just those who were addicted to alcohol or cocaine or heroin. My mission was to help others like myself who used anger like a drug. But first I had to recover from my own anger habit. I had to get my own act together.

Six years later I felt I had a good handle on my anger. I felt I understood. And I felt I was ready to share what I had learned with others.

Bill's Recovery

Bill Fleeman, founder of Pathways to Peace, Inc., and author of *The Pathways to Peace Anger Management Workbook*, comes from a twelve-step program background. Therefore, readers who are familiar with twelve-step programs such as Alcoholics Anonymous (AA) or Narcotics Anonymous (NA) will recognize some similarities between these programs and the Pathways to Peace anger management program. Also, anyone who has attended twelve-step meetings should feel very comfortable attending a Pathways to Peace anger management meeting because, structurally, the programs are similar. But Pathways to Peace is not a twelve-step program. What it does have is a set of eight principles that Pathways to Peace members use as guidelines for recovery from abusive anger.

My personal recovery involved an eight-step process. Later these eight steps became the Eight Principles of Pathways to Peace. You will find all of the Pathways to Peace Principles defined in Appendix 1, starting on page 200.

First I did a self-assessment—an *honest* self-assessment. Others—my friends, the police, judges and psychiatrists—had told me I had a problem with anger, but I needed to find out for myself. It was the only way to break down my wall of denial.

I put the emphasis on *honesty* and did my self-assessment. It was my assessment, not someone else's, and through it I found I had a serious problem with anger and rage. Some authority figure I resented didn't do the assessment of me—I did. So I had to own the results. I admitted to a serious problem with anger, I admitted I had harmed other people, I admitted I had harmed property, and I admitted I had harmed myself. I could no longer deny the problem.

I admitted these things only to myself at first, later to others. Then I made apologies. In some cases I made restitution. That is, I repaid people for the damage I had done to their property.

I couldn't always apologize or repay, because I had done some of the damage long before. Also, some people I had hurt lived two thousand miles away or I had no way of reaching them. Sometimes I wrote letters and mailed them. Sometimes I wrote letters but did not mail them.

I made apologies and restitution in order to get beyond the guilt and shame. I had a lot of guilt and shame, even if I wasn't always aware of it, and I knew these feelings stood in my way. I had to deal with my guilt and shame, otherwise I could never fully recover. My apologies and restitution helped put the guilt and shame behind me.

Then I struggled with the idea of responsibility. In the past I had always blamed others. I would not own my behavior, and I would not own the negative results of my behavior. Blaming others had been part of my denial. Finally I saw I would have to own my behavior, and I would have to own the results. I knew I would not recover if I continued to blame.

Then another thing occurred to me: I would have to make a practical decision, and I would have to put it into action. I would have to *decide to stop* my harmful behavior, and then I would have to actually *stop* the behavior.

I also saw I must become willing to forgive those who had harmed me: my father who had abandoned me, the reformatory guard who had punched me in the spine, and others. I must also become willing to forgive myself for the harm I had done others. I knew willingness to forgive was important, that it would release my guilt, shame, and resentment. I knew these things kept me stuck.

My self-assessment made me confront my beliefs about violence. Before, I'd believed violence was often justified. You could take just so much, right? What if you reasoned and people wouldn't listen? What if you begged and people laughed in your face? What if you compromised and people took advantage of you? Wasn't violence justified then? And there were wars—wars against tyranny, wars against men like Hitler. Wasn't violence justified in those situations?

Then I discovered I wasn't asking the question the right way. I was asking about violence in a general way. I needed to ask myself the question in a personal way.

First I needed to make a self-statement based on my self-assessment. I needed to say, "I have an addiction. I am addicted to anger. I get drunk on anger and rage, and I harm others. Then I pay dues—I lose something." The question formed itself. I asked, "As an anger addict, can I ever justify violence?"

Finally I put all arguments aside. Maybe some people think violence is justified, and maybe they can afford to think so. But in good conscience I could not, not as a person addicted to anger. I then committed myself to the belief that violence in any form is never justified, *unless my life or that of a loved one is in danger.*

I had learned early on that anger made me feel powerful. I learned that on the school steps when I copped my first anger high at eight years old. My self-assessment showed I used anger to feel powerful. It also revealed that I ended up doing harm to others and to myself, and then I lost things like my freedom. My self-assessment also showed I must find new ways to feel powerful, and I must learn practical skills to deal with anger triggers. I made a sincere effort to learn ways to feel powerful, ways that did not violate other people's right to feel safe.

I knew others had harmed me in the past, sometimes cruelly. They had injured my body and mind. But that was not all—they also injured my dignity and self-respect. They injured my self-worth.

I saw that I passed those injuries on to others, using anger and rage to make others feel worthless. I robbed others of their dignity and self-respect. But now I saw they didn't deserve the pain I caused them, and now I wanted to change. I promised myself I would treat others with dignity and respect—no matter what had been done to me, no matter how others may have hurt me.

I learned I had many negative, limiting beliefs that had kept me stuck in anger and rage. I studied my beliefs and learned to identify the ones that kept me stuck. I learned how to let go of them, and then I learned new beliefs to take their place. My new, positive beliefs helped to change my angry behavior.

Before, I had thought I could not change. That was one of the beliefs that had kept me stuck. If I can't change, I'd reasoned, then why should I try? Also, I'd felt my life had no purpose, no meaning, which was yet another belief that had kept me stuck. If that were the case, I had asked myself, then why should I change? Finally I learned I did have the ability to change, and I learned I did have a purpose. These discoveries gave me hope.

I worked hard at this eight-step process, working the program as hard as I could. Basic changes started to happen, positive changes. Not only my behavior changed, but my attitude, outlook, and character also changed. I was personally transformed. That transformation continues today.

I forgave those who'd harmed me and forgave myself for the harm I had done to others. I committed myself to helping others recover from anger addiction. I now continue my personal program of emotional, mental, and spiritual growth.

I wrote down my story, and then told my story to someone else. Sharing my story helped me heal and I knew this process could also help others heal.

Now my purpose was clear. I had a mission. My mission was to continue my own recovery and to help other people who had problems with anger and rage. But I needed a way to deliver the goods; I needed a vehicle to help others recover. It came to me in a flash: I would create a self-help movement called Pathways to Peace to empower angry people to help themselves change. I wrote the *The Pathways to Peace Anger Management Workbook*. Then I took the show on the road. Now Pathways to Peace groups are popping up all over the country.

Moving On to Your Story

While you read Bill's story, you may have thought about similar events in your own life. Again, the purpose of reading Bill's story is not to compare whose story is "better" or "worse," but to explore the feelings that often come up regarding anger. The following exercises are meant to help you look at your own story and think about your own feelings concerning anger and rage.

◆ **EXERCISE 1** Bill says he was an infant when his father left him, and that made him feel later that there was something wrong with him, that he felt defective. Did anything happen in your life to make you feel that way? Did you ever feel there was something "wrong" with you? Describe that feeling and how it affected you.

_____

_____

_____

_____

_____

_____

◆ **EXERCISE 2** Bill saw violent acts in his home from an early age. Did you see violence in your home when you were growing up? How did you feel about the violence you saw? How did you react to it?

_____

_____

_____

_____

_____

_____

◆ **EXERCISE 3** Bill lost his grandfather when he was five and he thought his grandfather's death was his fault. Did you lose someone important in your life as a child? Or as an adult? If you did, how did that make you feel?

_____

_____

_____

_____

◆ **EXERCISE 4** Bill said he felt his first "anger high" when he was eight years old. How old were you when you felt your first anger high? What happened? Did you hurt someone? Did you get hurt? Did you suffer negative results?

_____

_____

_____

_____

◆ **EXERCISE 5** Bill said he never felt he belonged and never felt accepted. Did you ever feel that way? Bill said he joined a gang and that for the first time ever he felt safe and he felt he belonged. Did you ever join a gang? If you did, how did it make you feel?

_____

_____

_____

_____

◆ **EXERCISE 6** Bill said he got into serious trouble as a teenager because of his anger. Did you get into serious trouble as a teenager because of your anger? How did you feel when you got into trouble because of your anger?

_____

_____

_____

_____

_____

◆ **EXERCISE 7** Bill drank too much and developed a problem with alcohol. Later he became addicted to other drugs as well. Bill said alcohol and other drugs made his anger worse. Do alcohol or other drugs make your anger worse?

_____

_____

_____

_____

◆ **EXERCISE 8** Bill was once hospitalized for depression. Have you ever suffered from bouts of depression because of things you have done when angry? What happened as a result of your depression? How did you come out of it, if you did?

_____

_____

_____

_____

◆ **EXERCISE 9** Bill said he finally found out what was wrong: He found he was addicted to anger. He said anger was like a drug to him. Have you found out what is wrong? What do you think about Bill's statement that anger is like a drug?

_____

_____

_____

_____

_____

LESSON 2 ~ The Importance of Self-Honesty

Self-honesty is crucial, because if your assessment is dishonest then it will be inaccurate. You must be honest with yourself right from the start. It is the one requirement in the self-assessment process. You must not lie to yourself.

Watch for three pitfalls that will trip you up and make self-honesty impossible. They will cause you to lie to yourself. Then you will fall into the trap of denial. Watch for:

1. **Rationalizing:** To "rationalize" means to make excuses. You are rationalizing when you say things like, "He (or she) wouldn't leave me alone. He (or she) just kept at me. That's why I screamed at (or hit) him (or her)."

◆ **EXERCISE** Think of a situation where you became angry. How did you make excuses for your angry behavior? Write down three examples.

_____

_____

_____

_____

_____

_____

2. **Minimizing:** Minimizing means lying to yourself about how angry you get, or lying to yourself about how often you get angry. "I never get too angry." "I only get angry once in a while." These are examples of minimizing.

◆ **EXERCISE** How have you used minimizing to defend your angry behavior? Write down three examples.

_____

_____

_____

_____

_____

_____

3. **Blaming:** Blaming means lying to yourself about responsibility. It means telling others it is their fault. "My father used to beat me up when I was a kid, for no reason. It is his fault I am so angry now." That is an example of blaming.

◆ **EXERCISE** How have you used blaming to defend your angry behavior? Write down three examples.

_____

_____

_____

_____

_____

_____

LESSON 3 ~ Writing Your Story

Write your story, using Bill's story as a guide. Tell about your childhood. Tell about how you developed your anger problem. Tell about the things you did when angry. Tell about your results. Tell about the dues you had to pay. Finally, tell about how things are now.

Your story will, of course, go on, as you continue to change and grow. You will learn more about anger, and you will learn many new ways to change. Bill's story is not complete either, because he continues to learn, change, and grow. It is an ongoing process.

Some Important Points to Remember as You Write Your Story

1. Don't worry about spelling, grammar, or punctuation. Just get your story down on paper. That's the only important thing.

2. Writing your story might bring up bad memories and bad feelings. If that happens, talk things over with somebody. Talk to a friend or get some counseling. Then finish your story.

◆ **EXERCISE 1** In this exercise you will write your own story. Use the outline provided on the following pages.

A Message from Stone

Hi, my name is Stone. I'm a Native American from New Mexico. This is a small part of my story.

While in prison for a crime of rage, I was stabbed in the neck, leg, and hand and almost died. My wounds were bad. I spent many days in the prison hospital. Usually I was the attacker; this time I was the one attacked. I remember lying there in the hospital ward. There was no noise. There were no screams. I had a chance to get some good sleep, and I didn't have to watch my back.

This stabbing was actually a blessing in my life. It took me out of circulation. It gave me a chance to take a look at my life and to dig up the roots of my anger and rage. I had a lot of time to think about where I was headed. That opened a door for me to work on some stuff that had held me hostage from being the human being I really am inside. Anger and rage had eaten me up and destroyed my life. I decided I wasn't going to let it take over my life anymore, and keep me stuck. I decided I wasn't going to let it keep me from my sacred purpose.

Writing my story was hard. It made me think about things I didn't want to think about. I wrote my story down because I knew it could help someone else. That's why I'm telling part of my story here. Maybe it'll help you.

✎ My Story ✎

My Childhood

Where I was born... _____

_____

_____

_____

_____

_____

My father and mother... _____

_____

_____

_____

_____

_____

_____

_____

_____

_____

_____

_____

_____

Bad things that happened to me and how they made me feel... _____

_____

_____

_____

_____

_____

_____

_____

_____

_____

Good things that happened to me and how they made me feel... _____

_____

_____

_____

_____

_____

_____

_____

_____

_____

_____

_____

Bad things that happened to me and how they made me feel... _____

_____

_____

_____

_____

_____

_____

_____

_____

Good things that happened to me and how they made me feel... _____

_____

_____

_____

_____

_____

_____

_____

_____

_____

_____

My first anger high... _____

_____

_____

_____

_____

_____

_____

_____

_____

_____

My first consequences... _____

_____

_____

_____

_____

_____

_____

_____

_____

_____

_____

My Adulthood

Bad things that happened to me and how they made me feel... _____

_____

_____

_____

_____

_____

_____

_____

_____

Good things that happened to me and how they made me feel... _____

_____

_____

_____

_____

_____

_____

_____

_____

How my angry behavior has already improved... _____

_____

_____

_____

_____

_____

_____

_____

_____

My Future

Changes I would like to make in my behavior and character in the future...

_____

_____

_____

_____

_____

_____

_____

_____

Where I want to be... _____

_____

_____

_____

_____

_____

_____

_____

_____

What I want to accomplish... _____

_____

_____

_____

_____

_____

_____

_____

_____

_____

_____

_____

_____

How I want to be remembered... _____

_____

_____

_____

_____

_____

_____

_____

_____

◆ **EXERCISE 2** You have written your story, which is a very important step in the healing process you have begun. Now it is time to tell your story to someone else, and the sooner the better. Sharing your story will help you heal more quickly by helping you move beyond the guilt and shame. In fact, share your story now. But choose carefully the person you will tell it to. Make sure you choose someone who will take you seriously. Choose someone who will understand what you are trying to do. Choose someone who is not emotionally linked to you and who will not judge you. For example, sharing your story with your spouse is not a good idea, especially if you have hurt him or her with your anger. Explain to the person who is listening that telling your story is a major part of your recovery from your anger problem. Explain that he or she need only listen to your story. Explain that you would rather not have him or her comment or give you feedback.

You might consider telling your story to a professional counselor, especially if your story contains some shockers. Perhaps you are a member of Pathways to Peace. Then you might want to read your story to your Pathways to Peace mentor. You might choose a minister or priest. Your spouse or partner may not be a good choice.

Who will you tell your story to?

_____

_____

Now you are ready to do your self-test. It will complete your self-assessment.

Read the questions and check the "yes" or "no" box following each question. Be as honest as you can.

	Yes	No
1. Have you ever harmed anyone because of anger?	☐	☐
2. Have you ever harmed a loved one when angry?*	☐	☐
3. Have you ever harmed yourself when angry?*	☐	☐
4. Have you ever lost a job because of anger?*	☐	☐
5. Have you often felt guilt or remorse after getting angry?	☐	☐
6. Has a significant other ever threatened to leave because of your anger?*	☐	☐
7. Were you ever arrested where anger was a factor?*	☐	☐
8. Have you often felt unable to control your anger?	☐	☐
9. Has a friend or loved one said you have a problem with anger?	☐	☐
10. Has a counselor or therapist said you have a problem with anger?	☐	☐

How to Score the Test

A "yes" answer to just one of the ten questions shows a problem with anger. A "yes" answer to any of the questions marked with an asterisk (*) shows a serious problem with anger.

Have you been honest with yourself? Did the test show you have an anger problem? If so, please study the agreement on the next page carefully. You are urged to sign the agreement before going on to Chapter 2. It is an agreement you make with yourself. It is proof of your desire to change. It is a promise to yourself.

Anti-Violence Self-Agreement

Anti-violence means you are against violence. *Self-agreement* means you make an agreement with yourself. If you did an honest self-assessment, you know whether or not you have a problem with anger. If your assessment revealed a problem, then you know you must change your behavior. Are you serious about changing your violent behavior? If you are, consider the fourteen-point self-agreement below. Look it over closely. Think about it. Then decide.

But don't enter into this agreement lightly. It is an agreement you make with yourself. If you violate the agreement, you violate yourself, not someone else. If you decide to sign this agreement, have it witnessed. Sign it in the presence of someone you like and admire. And have that person sign as witness.

I, _____, enter into the following agreement with myself:

1. I agree to admit I have a problem with anger.
2. I agree to admit I have harmed others, property, or myself.
3. I agree to apologize or make restitution, wherever possible, to those I harmed.
4. I agree to accept personal responsibility for the results of my actions.
5. I agree to decide to stop my harmful behavior.
6. I agree to become willing to forgive those who harmed me.
7. I agree to become willing to forgive myself for the harm I have done others.
8. I agree I have used violence to feel powerful over people, situations, and things.
9. I agree my violence has never been justified and will never be justified.
10. I agree to learn nonviolent ways to have feelings of personal power.
11. I agree not to violate other people's right to feel safe in their person and property.
12. I agree to treat all people and their property with respect and dignity.
13. I agree to let go of old beliefs that have kept me stuck in anger and violence.
14. I agree to search for the purpose of my life and to grow toward that purpose.

Date: _____

Signature: _____ Witness: _____

The agreement you signed and had witnessed is not just words on paper. It is a binding document. It is a pact with yourself. Signing it means you have made a sincere commitment. You agree to fulfill all of the terms. If you break this agreement, who will know? You will know. The witness you like and admire will know. Having signed the self-contract, you may now feel a little uneasy. You may be wondering what you should do next. Go on and finish the rest of the workbook. It will help you learn new ways to deal with anger so that you can keep the agreement you've made with yourself.

2

Understanding the Nature of Anger, Rage, and Violence

In Chapter 1 you completed a self-assessment to find out if you have an anger problem. Now it's time to find out what, exactly, is the nature of the problem.

Normal Anger

All people get angry, but not all people have a serious problem with anger. In fact, most people do not. Most people express anger in ways that do not seriously harm other people physically or emotionally. They do not harm animals or property. They do not harm themselves. They do not use anger as a primary tool of power and control. Most people use anger only once in a while, and they do not suffer negative results because of anger.

Addictive Anger

Some people have a serious problem with anger. They have developed an *anger habit*. In some cases, the habit has turned into an addiction. They do serious physical or emotional harm to other people, to animals, to property, or to themselves. They use anger as a primary tool for power and control. They use anger often, and they suffer serious personal consequences. They go to jail, lose their families, and often they become victims themselves. Sometimes they are seriously injured or even killed by other angry people.

Resentment and Hate

Resentment and hate are forms of anger. Resentment is a milder form, while hate is the most intense form of anger.

31

A Message from Luis

Hi, my name is Luis. I'm from Toledo, Ohio. I'm a third-generation American. My great-grandmother and great-grandfather were from Puerto Rico, but I was born here. I go to a Pathways to Peace group to work on my anger. But lately it's been real hard. Following the suicide attacks on the United States on September 11, 2001, something happened that made me feel even more fear and more anger than I felt when I heard about the New York City and Washington, D.C., attacks.

Three days after the suicide attacks, I was at my job at a gas station where I'm a mechanic. I was helping out at the pumps that day. Everybody was topping off their tanks because they thought we were going to run out of gas. A guy in a pickup truck pulled in. I went out to ask him how much gas he wanted. When I got to the side of his truck, the guy pulled out a gun. He pointed the gun right at my face. I didn't know what to do. The guy's hand was shaking, too. I was scared, man! I thought I was going to die right there, and I couldn't figure out why. Then the guy swore at me and called me a name. He said, "Why don't all you sand niggers go back to Egypt!" Then I understood. I said, "Look, I'm not even from an Arab country. I'm an American. My family's been here for a long time, but some of my family were born in Puerto Rico. I'm not from Egypt or Saudi Arabia or any other Arab country."

The guy's face got red. He apologized. He stuck the gun back in his belt and burned rubber getting out of there. Man, I was scared! I've got brown skin and black hair that's sort of straight. The guy had mistaken me for an Arab American. It gave me a different slant on racial and religious hate, though; I can tell you that. I found out what real Arab Americans had to go through. Not long after that, I heard about a real Arab American who worked in a gas station in Texas. He got shot by someone just like the guy that stuck the gun in my face, and he died.

People who use anger and rage in order to feel powerful over people, places, and things often hate individuals and groups simply because they are different. Sometimes people from different racial or ethnic groups are targets for their hate. Other times, people who have a different sexual orientation or people who have different religious beliefs are targeted.

Hate Crimes

All criminal acts committed simply on the basis of race, ethnicity, sexual orientation, or religious belief are called *hate crimes*. A recent example of a hate crime occurred 11 September 2001, when suicide bombers hijacked three commercial airliners and used them as missiles to attack the World Trade Center in New York City and the Pentagon building in Washington, D.C. A fourth airliner was highjacked but failed to reach its target when passengers apparently fought with the attackers and forced the plane to crash in a field near Pittsburgh, Pennsylvania.

The suicide attacks on 11 September 2001 killed more than 3,000 people. The primary motive for the attacks was ethnic, racial, and religious hate. The perpetrators were radical Muslim fundamentalists of Arab descent who hated Americans because, as a group, Americans have different religious beliefs and are generally of a different ethnicity. Of course, socio-economic factors and politics were involved as well, but the events of that day still fit the definition of hate crimes.

Following the attacks, some angry U.S. citizens vented their rage on Muslim Americans and Arab Americans who had nothing to do with the attack and who were as traumatized by it as everyone else. Then various fundamentalist religious groups in the United States jumped on the bandwagon of hate. Fanning the flames of hatred even more, they said God had stopped protecting America and was, instead, punishing all Americans because of feminists, homosexuals, abortionists, civil rights groups, and other liberal secular agencies and organizations.

Road Rage

Road rage is another dangerous form of anger. Road rage incidents are published in the newspapers every day. People who get involved in road rage incidents are often people who have been chronically angry for years, perhaps for most of their lives. Some episodes of road rage result in death. Sometimes people who express road rage shoot and kill other drivers. Sometimes they use their cars as weapons, crashing into other people's cars. Sometimes they kill whole families. Often the occupants of both cars end up dead.

The triggers for road rage are the same as for other forms of anger and rage: emotions that make the angry person feel powerless. Two examples of feelings or emotions that make people feel powerless are 1) disrespect and 2) fear. The person expressing road rage may feel disrespected or endangered when another driver cuts him or her off. Some people who have an anger problem use road rage as their primary way of expressing anger. However, the consequences for this kind of anger can be very serious. Not only can road rage lead to serious injury or death, most states now recognize road rage as a crime. People found guilty of crimes where road rage is a factor may receive long prison terms.

◆ **EXERCISE 1** Do you have an anger habit, or even an anger addiction? Check "Yes" or "No."

☐ Yes   ☐ No

◆ **EXERCISE 2** Have you used racial or ethnic groups as targets for your anger? Have you used people with a different sexual preference or different religious belief as targets for your anger? Explain any such incidents.

_____

_____

_____

_____

_____

_____

◆ **EXERCISE 3** How do the laws in your state treat hate crimes? Have you ever been a victim of a hate crime or felt you were unfairly singled out because of another person's prejudices? If so, how did that make your feel?

_____

_____

_____

_____

_____

◆ **EXERCISE 4** Have you ever expressed anger through road rage? If so, what kinds of consequences have you experienced?

_____

_____

_____

_____

LESSON 2 ~ What Is Violence?

Visualize a line stretching from wall to wall across a room. The line runs from left to right. The left-hand wall represents verbal abuse. Verbal abuse includes name-calling, screaming and yelling, threats, and sarcasm. Threatening postures and gestures combined with verbal abuse are somewhere in the middle of the line. The right-hand wall represents physical violence that may result in injury or death. _It is all violence._

V   I   O   L   E   N   C   E

◀ _Verbal Abuse ~ Violent Threats/Postures ~ Physical Violence_ ▶

A Message from Raymond

My name is Raymond. I'm from Arizona. I always thought I had a normal amount of anger. But I grew up in a house where somebody was angry every day. There was a lot of screaming and yelling. Sometimes there was hitting and sometimes things were broken. That's what I saw and heard in my house. I didn't have anything to compare it to. So, to me, it was normal.

◆ **EXERCISE 1** What kinds of violence have you used?

_____

_____

_____

_____

_____

◆ **EXERCISE 2** Have you ever been the target of physical violence? If so, how did it make you feel?

_____

_____

_____

_____

◆ **EXERCISE 3** Have you been a victim of verbal violence? If so, how did that make you feel?

_____

_____

_____

_____

A Message from Jack

Hi, everybody. My name is Jack, and I abuse anger. I'm also addicted to alcohol and to some other drugs, too. But I've been clean and sober for quite a few years now.

If you've never had an alcohol or drug hangover, then you won't understand how anger is like a drug, the way I can understand it. But you can get some idea. It's easy for me; I've had hundreds of hangovers, maybe thousands. I had one hangover that lasted three days! I didn't think I was going to live. Tequila and downers caused that one. I never had an anger hangover that lasted three days, but I had some that were pretty bad. They felt just like alcohol hangovers. They made me feel totally drained. I'd wake up in the morning feeling guilty as hell and stupid, too. The difference was, I could always remember what I did and why I felt guilty. That's why I felt stupid the morning after an anger binge. That's why, to me, anger hangovers are worse than alcohol and drug hangovers. With alcohol and drug hangovers, you don't always remember what you did and said.

Anger is *like* a drug, and you can develop an anger habit the way some people develop a drug habit. You can even become addicted to anger. Strong anger has a "speedball" effect. It is like using cocaine, then using heroin immediately afterward. The angry outburst is like a cocaine rush, making you feel powerful. Then when the anger subsides, you feel a sense of relief that is like the very relaxed feeling produced by heroin.

Here's how you develop an anger habit or addiction: You use anger over and over, and experience a "high" each time you use it. The brain enjoys the high and wants to repeat it, and so you continue getting high on anger over and over again. Finally you develop an anger habit because you get addicted to the high produced by the anger.

Drug addicts develop a high tolerance to their drug. They need more and more of the drug to feel high. High tolerance is a hallmark of addiction.

Alcoholics are addicted to the drug called alcohol. They develop a high tolerance for alcohol. They also suffer a rebound effect from the drug. They feel hungover, shaky, and tired the next day; they feel guilt, shame, and free-floating fear.

Angry people get drunk on anger. Like alcoholics, they develop a high tolerance to their drug, anger. They need to use more and more anger to feel high. Like alcoholics, they suffer a rebound effect. Anger addicts have anger and rage hangovers. They feel shaky and tired the morning after; they feel guilt, shame, and free-floating fear.

◆ **EXERCISE 1** How are anger and rage like a drug?

_____

_____

_____

◆ **EXERCISE 2** Strong anger has a "speedball" effect. What does that mean?

_____

_____

_____

_____

◆ **EXERCISE 3** Have you ever felt "hungover" the morning after an anger binge? Describe how you felt.

_____

_____

_____

_____

LESSON 4 ~ Excessive Anger as Learned Behavior

You did not have to learn _how to be_ angry, but you did have to learn to _abuse_ anger.

You were born with the ability to use anger. You used that ability as an infant—if you were hungry, you felt discomfort, and if you weren't fed, you got frustrated. The hunger and frustration triggered your anger. You yelled and cried, kicked and screamed, and then someone fed you. Or you went to sleep. If you went to sleep hungry, you probably woke up angry again. Later you learned other ways to get your needs met. You didn't forget how to use anger, but you learned other ways to deal with hunger, and you learned other ways to deal with frustration and other anger triggers.

Somewhere along the way, your anger got out of control. It became a pattern, a habit. You used anger more and more to deal with the world. You began abusing anger. The more you used anger, the more you wanted to use it. The more you used it, the more you forgot how to use other ways to get your needs met. Your anger got out of control, the way an alcoholic's drinking gets out of control.

How Did You Learn Your Anger Habit?

You learned your anger habit from other people. You may have learned it from one or both of your parents, or from your brothers or sisters. You probably learned some of the pattern from kids you grew up with. You learned it from what you saw and heard others do. You learned some of your anger from television and movies, and from books and video games.

You learned a major part of your pattern from the results you got when you used anger. You felt pleasure when you got angry. You felt powerful. You copped a high. You recorded the high in your memory, in the pleasure center of your brain. The memory of the high was etched deeper in memory each time you felt it.

You probably didn't suffer strong negative results in the beginning; if you had, you probably wouldn't have developed an anger habit in the first place. You used angry behavior to feel powerful, and it worked. You didn't lose anything. You didn't go to jail and lose your freedom, and you didn't get hurt. You used anger and received only pleasure, never pain. You were consistently rewarded with pleasure; that's how you learned much of your anger problem.

You were not born with an anger and rage problem, and you are not "sick." Your problem is not a result of bad genetics. Your problem is a result of faulty learning. It is not up to society to "cure" you. You are responsible for your anger. It is up to you to change yourself.

◆ **EXERCISE** How did you learn your anger problem? Who and what taught you to use anger to get what you want?

_____

_____

_____

_____

_____

_____

_____

_____

_____

On the Surface—Outward Focus

Some people express anger openly—that is, their anger is on the surface. They are loud and aggressive and they direct their anger outward, at other people. The results they suffer are also obvious. They hurt others, they go to jail, or they get beat up. Sometimes they hurt themselves.

◆ **EXERCISE** Do you use the surface style of anger? If so, how do you express your anger? What kind of consequences have you suffered?

_____

_____

_____

_____

Underwater—Inward Focus

Other people use what is called the *underwater style.* They express their anger inwardly. They aren't as likely to say or do things to other people and they aren't as likely to damage property. The negative results they suffer are less apparent: They develop ulcers. They often have high blood pressure. They often suffer severe bouts of depression. Sometimes they do physical harm to themselves.

◆ **EXERCISE** Do you use the underwater style of anger? If so, how do you express your anger? What kind of results have you experienced?

_____

_____

_____

_____

"Justified" and "Righteous" Anger

The recovering alcohol addict understands getting drunk on alcohol is never justified. The recovering anger addict understands that getting drunk on anger is never justified, no matter how righteous the cause. *If you are recovering from an anger habit or an anger addiction, you must understand that getting drunk on anger is **never** justified, no matter how righteous the cause.*

◆ **EXERCISE** Why is anger and rage never justified, no matter how righteous the cause?

_____

_____

_____

_____

Sarcastic Anger

Sarcasm is a mask. Don't be fooled. Sarcasm is anger. It causes harm by hurting people's feelings. It is an unfair power play. Using sarcasm reinforces violent behavior.

◆ **EXERCISE** Do you use sarcasm? Have you ever been the target of sarcasm? If so, how did it make you feel?

_____

_____

_____

_____

Humorous, Teasing, and "Button-Pushing" Anger

Anger is often disguised as humor. Making jokes at somebody else's expense is an example of anger disguised as humor. Some angry people use teasing or "button-pushing" to hurt others. You are using button-pushing when you deliberately say or do things that you know will cause a strong reaction.

◆ **EXERCISE 1** Do you disguise your anger with humor? Do you do "funny" things that in some way hurt others? Do you say "funny" things that cause others emotional pain?

_____

_____

_____

_____

_____

◆ **EXERCISE 2** Do you tease people or use button-pushing to hurt other people?

_____

_____

_____

_____

_____

A Message from Brenda

I didn't know it was _all_ violence. I didn't know how much power words have. I didn't know how much damage words could do. I didn't know how much pain my screaming and yelling caused my kids. I didn't know how much damage my sarcasm caused. Maybe on some level, I knew. Later when I started getting a handle on my anger problem, I remembered that people said things to me when I was a kid that really hurt. I remembered how words damaged my self-esteem. My family said things. My mother sometimes called me stupid. "You're stupid, Brenda!" she'd scream. Every time she said it, it felt like a knife in my heart. Then my brother and sister would get in on it too. "Yeah. You're stupid, Brenda!" they'd yell. Teachers said things; other kids said things. Later, that type of anger became a part of my anger problem. After a while I got real sensitive to words, and I got real good at using words like knives to cut people. Finally I became aware of what I was doing. I'm still struggling with my anger, but I don't use words in anger to hurt people anymore. Especially my kids.

A Message from Al

Hi. I'm Al, and I'm an anger addict. When I was seven, my mother died in a car accident. I went through the denial stage of the grief process within a few days. Then the anger set in, and I got stuck there. Oh, I did some bargaining, too. I tried to make a bargain with God. I said I'd never do anything bad ever again if only my mom would come back. Then the depression started. I didn't know what to do about that, so I jumped back into anger. That worked; it got me out of the depression. Every time I started to feel depressed, I'd get angry instead. My anger caused me problems in school, and with family and friends. But I didn't care; at least I wasn't depressed anymore. I had bad consequences because of my angry behavior, but the trade-off seemed like a good deal.

Finally, I got some counseling. It was years later, but at last I understood what was going on. I got some insight from the counseling. I went to some anger-management classes. I changed my behavior for the better. Things in my life got a lot better, too!

You may never identify a specific event in your life that prompted your anger habit. But some people do experience a specific event, and recognizing that trigger event is very helpful in moving away from an anger habit. One thing that can set off an anger habit is loss of a loved one.

Grief means "deep sorrow." When you *grieve*, you suffer strong feelings of *loss*.

If someone you love—a parent, child, spouse, or close friend—dies, you suffer grief. The death of a loved one is a great loss. If someone you love leaves you—by moving away, abandonment, or divorce—you also grieve. Any time you lose something you greatly value, you suffer grief. For example, when alcoholics and drug addicts stop using alcohol and drugs, they also suffer grief. They grieve the loss of their drug(s) of choice.

The Grief Process

Grief is more than *deep sorrow;* grief is a process. All people go through the same process when they grieve the loss of someone or something they love or greatly value. You may have lost a parent or loved one because that person died or because of abandonment or divorce. You may have lost a job or career you loved. You may have lost a great deal of money. You may have lost your self-respect because of something you did. Losses such as these would undoubtedly cause you to suffer grief.

According to Elizabeth Kübler-Ross's book *On Death and Dying,* a good book for people going through the grieving process, there are five stages in the grief process: denial, anger, bargaining, depression, and acceptance. The first stage in the grief process is called *denial.* When you lose something you greatly value, at first you can't believe it happened; you want to deny the loss. The denial stage of the grief process usually passes quickly. The second stage, *anger,* is discussed in detail below. The *bargaining* stage usually passes fairly quickly, too, but the *depression* stage may last a long time. It can take one to three years to reach the *acceptance* stage of the grief process. But sometimes people get stuck in the process. Of course, it is worth noting that the grief process is not linear. People can move from one stage to another in any order.

◆ The Anger Stage

The second stage of the grief process is *anger*. In this stage, you see that the loss is real. You see that it really happened, and that makes you *angry*. You may even *rage* at the loss. The anger stage of the grief process can last days, or even months. In fact, the anger stage of the grief process can last years.

You may have suffered a great loss at some time in the past. Notice that one of the stages of the grief process is *depression*. Depression is an anger trigger because it makes you feel powerless. You may be stuck in the anger stage of the grief process. You may have been using anger for a very long time, to fight depression due to grief. It may be the reason you developed an anger habit to begin with.

You do not have to stay stuck in the grief process. You can get grief counseling to help you move through the process. If you want help finding a grief counselor in your area, call the Pathways to Peace national office. The national office's contact number is on page 209 of this workbook. Learning to deal with the anger stage of the grief process will help you accept your loss, and then you can move on with your life.

◆ **EXERCISE 1** When do people suffer grief?

_____

_____

_____

_____

_____

_____

◆ **EXERCISE 2** Name the five stages of the grief process.

_____

_____

_____

_____

_____

◆ **EXERCISE 3** Have you suffered the loss of a loved one through death, divorce, or abandonment? Are you a recovering alcoholic or drug addict who is grieving the loss of your drug of choice? Write down your losses.

_____

_____

_____

_____

_____

◆ **EXERCISE 4** Why are people who are stuck in the anger stage of the grief process apt to abuse anger?

_____

_____

_____

_____

_____

◆ **EXERCISE 5** If you are stuck in the anger stage of the grief process, what can you do about it?

_____

_____

_____

_____

LESSON 8 ~ The Roots of Anger, Rage, and Violence

Many people who develop an anger problem were abused as children. Some were beaten, some were raped, some were traumatized by things they saw. Many were abandoned by one or both parents. They felt rejected, afraid. They could not predict what was going to happen to them. Often they blamed themselves for what happened. They felt defective. Later these feelings became triggers for anger and rage.

The trauma suffered by some anger addicts during childhood can have lasting effects. The environment they lived in was like a war zone. There was constant tension in their lives. The constant tension raised their inner tension above the normal level. This higher level of inner tension became a permanent condition. The inner tension level of most people who have problems with anger and rage is often higher than normal. The higher-than-normal tension level contributes to the development of anger problems. People with anger problems learn to use anger to relieve the tension. The increased tension level also accounts for the high number of anger addicts who are also addicted to alcohol and other drugs.

You may be one of those who suffered trauma during childhood; your home may have been like a war zone. If so, you can point at these things as part of the cause of your excessive use of anger. *But you must avoid using an abusive childhood as an excuse for using violence and rage in the present.* No matter what was done to you in the past, you are responsible for what you do to others in the present, and you are responsible for the harm you have done to yourself.

A Message from Vince

This is Vince talking. I'm from New York. My anger goes back a long time, to when I was a kid. I'm thirty years old now.

My mom and dad fought all the time. That's about all I can remember about my childhood, the fights. My dad was the most violent, though sometimes my mom threw things at my dad. They never beat me, but watching and listening to them fight really got to me. They usually fought in the kitchen. My bedroom was off the kitchen, so I often woke up to the sound of my mother screaming and my father cursing. It scared me and wrecked my sleep. I still have trouble sleeping. The first fight I can remember, I was about age five. The fights seemed to get worse till I was about seven. I don't remember if the cops ever came to the house. They might have, but I don't remember. I can remember my mom getting more scared as time went by.

Then one night we went to the grocery store. It was dark when we got back into the car in the parking lot. My mom and dad got into an argument in the car. We were still parked. My dad slapped my mom in the face. She screamed at him not to do it again. My dad slapped her again. I was standing up in the back seat. I saw my mom reach into her purse. Then I saw she had a gun in her hand. The shiny black barrel caught the light of the street lamp that stood next to the car. My mom didn't say anything. I saw her point the gun at my dad, right at his head. I saw a bright orange flash, then another one, and I heard two loud explosions. My dad died instantly. I was seven years old.

A Message from Lisa

My name is Lisa. I'm from Denver. I had an anger habit. Later, my anger habit turned into an addiction to anger and rage.

I never suffered trauma. I had a "normal" childhood, whatever that is. I had two loving parents who stayed together. They argued sometimes, but never fought. My parents never abused me with words, and they never abused me physically. I never witnessed violence in my home. I didn't have violent friends. I didn't watch a lot of violent movies and didn't play violent video games. I was never a victim of violence, yet I got addicted to anger. How come?

A recovering anger addict called Barbara is my mentor. She explained it to me this way. She said there are two types of anger addicts. One type is kind of set up for anger problems, because of things that happened to them or because of things they saw. Barbara said anger addicts who grew up in violent surroundings fit into this group. They feel powerless and use anger to feel powerful. They get addicted to anger fast.

The second type of anger addict is different. Barbara told me they don't come from violent homes. They have never had trauma in their lives. They come from normal homes. This type of anger addict doesn't start out feeling as powerless as the first type. They don't have as much fear and tension. They don't get addicted to anger as fast as the first group. But this type does find out that anger makes them feel high. They repeat the behavior over and over; finally, they get hooked on the high. They get addicted to the adrenaline rush. My mentor Barbara says I fit into that group.

There is no excuse for violence. You do not have to resolve your childhood issues in order to change, if you *want* to change. But someday you must forgive those who harmed you, and you must forgive yourself. This workbook will prepare you for that.

Although many anger addicts have experienced trauma at some time in their lives, some people develop an addiction to anger and rage without having suffered physical or emotional abuse of any kind.

PART TWO

Understand the Process of Recovery

3

The Eight Parts of
the Whole Self

Having read the material and completed the exercises in Chapter 2, you now have a deeper understanding of the nature of anger and rage. This chapter will introduce you to a key concept and add more depth to your understanding.

Your whole self is made up of eight parts. The eight parts are interactive and interdependent. Each part depends on the other seven parts, and each part acts on the other parts. How well all of the parts function will determine whether or not you fully recover from excessive anger and rage. You must change and grow in all of your eight parts in order to be happy in your recovery. The eight parts of your whole self are

1. the biological part: your body

2. the environmental part: your surroundings

3. the behavioral part: your actions, everything you do

4. the skill part: what you are good at, what you have learned

5. the values/goals part: what is important to you, what you want to be

6. the belief part: your attitudes about yourself and your world, what you believe to be true

7. the mission (identity) part: your purpose in life, why you are here

8. the spiritual part: the part of you that is connected to others, to the universe, and, if you like, to the God of your understanding

The Eight Parts of the Whole Self Compared to an Eight-Cylinder Car

One way to understand the eight parts of the whole self is by comparing the whole self to an eight-cylinder car. You are like an eight-cylinder car. To function fully and well, all eight cylinders must be in good shape. Each cylinder must cooperate and do its job. If all the cylinders cooperate, the car will take you where you want to go.

But what if one cylinder develops a problem? What if it becomes damaged? That cylinder will function poorly. The damaged cylinder will be unable to cooperate well with the rest of the cylinders. It will throw everything out of balance and cause the whole car to miss and lurch and lose power. Left unattended, the condition of the damaged cylinder will get worse and worse. Finally, the car will stop working altogether.

The damaged cylinder will have a negative effect on the rest of the cylinders. It will cause the other cylinders to work too hard. Soon another cylinder will develop problems, and then another and another. Finally the whole car will break down. The same is true of the recovery process. Full recovery means recovery of the whole self. It means recovery of all eight parts.

The Eight Parts of the Whole Self Compared to an Eight-Petaled Flower

Another way to understand the eight parts is by comparing the whole self to an eight-petaled flower. To be whole and healthy, all eight petals must be healthy. Each petal must cooperate, and do its job. If all the petals cooperate, the flower will thrive and grow.

But what if one petal becomes diseased? The diseased petal will function poorly. It will be unable to cooperate, unable to stay fully open along with the rest of the petals. If untreated, the diseased petal will close up. This will affect the rest of the petals. Soon they will close up, too, until the entire flower closes up like an angry fist. Then all light will be shut out; the flower will wilt. Closing up even tighter and tighter, the flower will eventually die.

◆ **EXERCISE 1** What happens to an eight-cylinder engine when one of the cylinders develops a problem? What happens when the problem goes untreated?

_____

_____

_____

_____

_____

_____

_____

_____

_____

◆ **EXERCISE 2** What does comparing the whole self to an eight-cylinder engine, or to an eight-petaled flower, have to do with understanding the recovery process?

_____

_____

_____

_____

_____

_____

LESSON 1 ~ The Biological Part

A Message from Don

I'm Don. I'm an anger addict. For years I damaged my body with booze and other drugs, like a lot of other anger addicts I know. I drank a lot of beer. I smoked a couple of packs of cigarettes a day. During some of those years, I exercised. Sometimes I ate right. From twenty-seven to thirty-five, I got way out of shape. I didn't exercise; I didn't eat right. I was sick with colds all winter. I developed high blood pressure. I had a beer gut. I didn't sleep well and was tired all the time. I looked ten years older than I was. Every time I looked in the mirror, my self-esteem plunged lower.

For me, low self-esteem was a major trigger. Finally I got clean and sober. I started exercising, eating right, and sleeping better. As soon as I got back into shape, I felt better about myself. Low self-esteem was not often a trigger after that.

Your health is determined by what you eat and by what you do with your body. Nutrition is an extremely important part of the process of recovery from an anger habit. A well-balanced diet of nutritious food will help to create a healthy body. A poorly balanced diet of junk food will create an unhealthy body. Overeating will cause you to gain weight, which may cause you to feel low self-esteem. Of course, not eating enough can also be injurious to your body and have a negative impact on your self-esteem. Feelings of low self-esteem can be a major anger trigger.

Your body also needs rest and sleep. You need six to nine hours of sleep each night in order to feel rested and alert. Just a day or two without adequate sleep will have a negative effect on how you feel and how you function. It will cause your tension level to rise. That will increase your sensitivity to frustration and anxiety, which are anger triggers.

Obviously, your body is important. If you are in good physical health, you feel good. When you feel good, you are more likely to use good behavior.

◆ **EXERCISE 1** What will happen if you don't pay attention to your body?

_____

_____

_____

_____

_____

◆ **EXERCISE 2** Name some things you could do that would improve the way you take care of your body.

_____

_____

_____

_____

LESSON 2 ~ The Environmental Part

You live in relationship to people, places, and things. The sum total of these people, places, and things is your _outer environment_. In fact, you could not live alone and stay alive. You could not survive without having certain people, places, and things in your life.

You choose the people, places, and things in your outer environment. The people, places, and things you choose affect the health of your body. They affect how you behave; they affect what skills you will develop; they affect your values and goals; they affect your beliefs; they affect your sense of mission; they affect your spirituality. People, places, and things

A Message from Bill

All of my friends were like me—addicted to anger. They came from the same kind of background I came from. They came from angry homes, alcoholic homes, abusive homes (I call these the three A's of unhappiness). When I started my recovery from anger addiction, I saw how much negative influence my old friends had on me. I saw the negative influence they had on my mind, on my thoughts, on my beliefs, my attitudes, and my values. Then I saw the negative influence certain places and things had on me. I stopped hanging out with my old friends; I stopped hanging out in the old places. And I stopped holding on to the old things.

affect all your parts. People, places, and things affect you in two ways: They affect you in a positive way, or they affect you in a negative way.

Your mind is another kind of environment, your *inner environment.* Your thoughts, spirituality, beliefs and attitudes, values and goals, and your automatic behaviors live in your mind. Your inner environment affects your outer environment. Your outer environment, in turn, affects your inner environment.

◆ **EXERCISE 1** List three people in your life who could have a negative influence on your recovery.

_____

_____

_____

◆ **EXERCISE 2** List three people in your life who could have a positive influence on your recovery.

_____

_____

_____

◆ **EXERCISE 3** List three places and three things in your life that could have a negative influence on your recovery.

_____

_____

_____

◆ **EXERCISE 4** List three places and three things in your life that could have a positive influence on your recovery.

_____

_____

_____

Behavior is action. If an action gives you pleasure, you will want to repeat it. If the action gives you strong pleasure, you may repeat it over and over no matter what.

When you repeat an action over and over again, you create a habit. Your actions become a part of you. In this way, you have created your anger and rage habit by repeating angry behavior. Fortunately, you can change your habits.

Recovery from your anger habit must start with behavior. You must stop your violent and angry behavior. You can't wait; you must do it now. If you do not change your behavior now, you will lose more things. You will lose more freedom, more relationships, more self-respect.

A Message from Peter

My name is Peter. I wanted to do it another way. I wanted to start with analyzing how I got addicted to anger in the first place. I spent a lot of time in counseling, searching for answers. Meanwhile, my behavior stayed the same. I needed some skills, some new ways to interrupt triggers. I needed to change my behavior; that's what I had to do first. Finding the causes could come later.

You must change in all parts of yourself, but you must change your angry behavior before you can change anything else. You have already signed the Anti-Violence Self-Agreement. Making positive changes, which are based on your answers from Lessons 1 and 2 in this chapter, will help you change your behavior.

◆ **EXERCISE 1** How did you use behavior to create your anger habit?

_____

_____

_____

_____

◆ **EXERCISE 2** What will happen if you don't change your angry behavior now?

_____

_____

_____

_____

A Message from Bill

I had some skills. I was a skilled weight lifter. I was a skilled machine operator and I had some art skills. But I didn't know how to manage my feelings. I didn't have those kinds of skills. I didn't know how to deal with embarrassment and anxiety and other negative feelings, except to get angry. In fact, anger was the only "skill" I had when it came to managing feelings. And, in a way, anger is a skill. It is something you learn by practicing angry behavior over and over. The problem is, it's a negative skill. When you use anger to deal with negative feelings, you have to pay dues.

You were not born with skills, but you were born with the ability to learn skills. Your ability to learn new skills makes it possible to change your angry behavior.

Your skills help you function; they help you obtain things you need or want. You have learned many skills during your life, and now you must learn new skills to deal with things that trigger your anger.

◆ **EXERCISE 1** Why do you need skills to recover from your anger habit?

_____

_____

_____

_____

_____

◆ **EXERCISE 2** List five important skills you have learned that help you in your life.

_____

_____

_____

_____

_____

A Message from Raul

My name is Raul. I live in Dallas and I'm a recovering anger addict.

I didn't know what values were, and I didn't care. I had no goals and didn't see why I should set any, so I had no idea what was really important in my life, and I had nothing to look forward to. I didn't know what to do or where to go. I felt like I was drifting in a boat in the ocean all alone, with no land in sight. I was scared. I felt lost and powerless, and that made me angry. Then I started my recovery from my anger habit. I learned about my values. I found out I felt good about myself when I was learning something, so learning became one of my top values. Then I found out about the importance of goals, and started to set some goals that would make me feel good. My main goal right now is to keep working on my anger. I also want to go to college. I'll have my high school diploma by next August; that's an important goal to me. I have an appointment to talk to the admissions people at the community college in September. That's another one of my important goals.

LESSON 5 ~ The Values/Goals Part

Values

Values and goals are closely connected. Values are the things and feelings that are important to you. Values tell you what things will give you pleasure, and they tell you what things will bring you pain. Values tell you what to move toward and what to move away from. Values also tell you what to think about. Values have a strong effect on your behavior. Your values even determine what skills you develop. They directly determine your goals. Your values have a strong effect on every other recovery level.

Full recovery from your anger habit requires you to look closely at your values. You will find you must change some of your values in order to recover. You will learn more about values in Chapter 12, later in the workbook.

Goals

Goals are plans for getting the things you want to have and want to do. Goals are plans for the future. You set goals in order to obtain things that will cause the pleasurable feelings you value. Goals reinforce your skills and help you make sense of your behavior. Your goals can even affect your body. Full recovery from your anger habit depends on your goals.

Goals and values give you reasons to keep growing and changing. They give you something to look forward to; they give you hope. You will learn more about goals in Chapter 15 of the workbook.

◆ **EXERCISE 1** What are values and what are they for?

_____

_____

_____

_____

_____

◆ **EXERCISE 2** Name at least three feelings you value.

_____

_____

_____

◆ **EXERCISE 3** Name at least three things you value.

_____

_____

_____

◆ **EXERCISE 4** What do goals do for you?

_____

_____

_____

_____

_____

◆ **EXERCISE 5** Do you have some goals? If so, name them.

_____

_____

_____

_____

_____

_____

LESSON 6 ~ The Beliefs Part

Your beliefs are one of the most powerful driving forces in your life. Beliefs are strong feelings about what you think is true or false or right or wrong.

You learn your beliefs from other people, including your parents, friends, and teachers. You learn some of your beliefs from books and movies. You learn your beliefs from things that happen to you. You have learned beliefs about yourself and about other people, and you have learned beliefs about the world. You have learned beliefs that are positive, and you have learned beliefs that are negative.

Your beliefs will have a powerful influence on whether you overcome your anger habit. Your beliefs give you the energy and the will to change. They deeply influence every other part of your whole self, and all other parts influence your beliefs.

In Chapter 13, you will learn more about beliefs. You will learn the difference between recovery beliefs and beliefs that keep you stuck. You will learn to become aware of your beliefs. You will learn the difference between positive and negative beliefs. You will learn how to change negative beliefs that limit you into positive beliefs that support your recovery from your anger habit.

◆ **EXERCISE 1** Name a belief you have about yourself. Is it a positive or negative belief?

_____

_____

_____

_____

◆ **EXERCISE 2** Name a belief you have about other people.

_____

_____

_____

_____

◆ **EXERCISE 3** Name a belief you have about the world.

_____

_____

_____

_____

LESSON 7 ~ The Mission Part

A complete identity includes a personal mission statement. Your mission statement is a description of your life purpose. Your personal mission is your reason for living, occupying space, doing, learning, feeling, acquiring things, believing, and being. Awareness of your personal mission will help you make sense out of everything else. It will help you stay focused on your main goal: recovery from your anger habit.

In Chapter 14, you will learn more about your mission. You will learn how to write down your mission statement so that you can use it to help you recover from your anger habit.

◆ **EXERCISE 1** What is a mission?

_____

_____

_____

_____

◆ **EXERCISE 2** Why is a sense of mission important to recovery from your anger habit?

_____

_____

_____

_____

_____

LESSON 8 ~ The Spiritual Part

All people have a spiritual part. You have a spiritual part, whether you know it or not. It is the part that helps you feel connected in a positive way to other people; to the universe; and to the God of your understanding, whatever that may mean to you in your overall view of the world. Pathways to Peace expects you to form your own understanding of the cosmos and your place in the grand scheme of things, because if you feel spiritually connected, you will discover a purpose even bigger than your personal mission. To fully recover and heal from your anger habit, you must pay attention to your spiritual part.

Of all the parts of the self, the spiritual part has the most power. When you develop a spiritual identity, it generates revolutionary change in all other parts of the self. *Revolutionary change* is big change. It can have a cascading effect that may lead to an overall transformation of all other recovery parts. **In fact, when change takes place at the spiritual part of the self, the rest of the self must change!** Dramatic personal change is almost always triggered by major change at the spiritual level.

A Message from John

I live in Los Angeles. My name is John. It was tough for me. My mother was a fundamentalist. She was also schizophrenic. Her disease caused her to interpret her religion in strange ways. She beat me when I was small. She said she did it to get the devil out of me. She said God told her to do it. She'd beat me, then she'd read the Bible to me. When I was twelve, they sent my mother to an asylum. I didn't become an atheist, but I angrily rejected God. I got hooked on violence. Anger and rage became my god. I got into trouble and paid a lot of dues before I started my recovery program. I stopped my violence, but I wasn't happy. My mentor told me I had to be nonviolent and happy, not just nonviolent. My mentor said I had to get spiritually connected. He said if I didn't, I wouldn't be happy. Then I would relapse back into violence, my drug of choice. So I started to open up my spiritual part. I did a lot of reading. I read about different religions and visited various churches. I'm still exploring, but I'm starting to form a healthy relationship with the God of my understanding; I'm starting to feel connected.

◆ **EXERCISE** Why is the spiritual part considered the most powerful of all the parts of the self?

_____

_____

_____

_____

_____

_____

_____

_____

_____

_____

4

The Eight Steps of
the Recovery Process

In Chapter 3, you learned that the "self" is organized into eight parts and that you must learn how to change and grow in all eight parts in order to be successful and happy in your recovery from your anger problem. In this chapter you will learn about the eight-step recovery process, and you will see that each recovery step is connected to one of the eight parts of the self.

Bill sees recovery from an anger habit as an eight-step process. It is one of the ways in which Bill chose to organize his thinking about recovery from chronic anger and helps to show how the Pathways to Peace anger management program differs from the twelve-step approach to change. Recovery from an anger habit is an eight-step process. The eight steps are based on the eight principles of Pathways to Peace. Remember the founder's story in Chapter 1? Remember what Bill said under the heading "Bill's Recovery"? Bill said he followed these same eight steps in order to recover from his addiction to anger and rage.

On the pages that follow, the eight steps you will need in order to recover from chronic anger are described in detail. There are also related exercises that will help you see how each step applies to you.

You must admit you caused harm, and you
must apologize and make restitution.

LESSON 1

First you did an honest self-assessment; now you must admit you caused harm. And wherever possible, you must apologize to the people you hurt. In some cases you will need to make restitution. That means you must pay for any damage you caused to someone's property.

Your primary purpose for apologizing is to help yourself deal with guilt and shame so that those feelings can no longer act as triggers. The apologies you make are for your benefit, but others may also benefit. The people you apologize or make restitution to will know you are trying to change.

The people you harmed may live far away, in which case you can apologize by letter. Sometimes you may find it impossible to apologize or make restitution, or you may think that it is inappropriate to contact a person. Sometimes, it's true, that it's better not to contact somebody you've harmed, because they may be trying to move on and away from their experiences with you. If so, you may not want to mail some of the letters of apology, but it's still important to write the apology down. That way, you, yourself, can read your apology and you can begin to heal.

Do the best you can as you work this step. Remember, this step is a part of a *process*. It isn't something you can do in one sitting. Talk to your Pathways to Peace mentor, or a counselor or a friend you trust, about whether you should actually contact somebody from your past. You will want to continue working this step throughout your recovery.

◆ **EXERCISE 1** Have you completed your self-assessment? Have you admitted you have a problem?

_____

_____

_____

_____

_____

_____

_____

◆ **EXERCISE 2** To whom will you apologize first? What will you say? How can you make restitution?

_____

_____

_____

_____

_____

◆ **EXERCISE 3** How will apologizing and making restitution help you in your recovery?

_____

_____

_____

_____

_____

◆ **EXERCISE 4** Make a list of at least five people you have harmed.

_____

_____

_____

_____

_____

_____

You must accept responsibility for your actions.
You must decide to stop your harmful behavior and become
willing to forgive others and yourself.

LESSON 2

You did not take responsibility for your actions in the past; instead, you blamed others, like Bill did. Now you must "own" your behavior, and you must "own" the results of your behavior. In order to fully recover and heal from your anger habit, you must stop blaming.

A good example of how you are already taking responsibility for your actions is the self-agreement you signed at the end of Chapter 1. That is a good start, but now you are responsible for following through. What if you break your agreement? The agreement means you are now accountable for your behavior, so if you break it, you must get back on track.

Other people have hurt you. Holding on to these hurts keeps you angry. This is called *resentment*. Also, you have done things that have hurt others, and you probably feel some guilt and shame. You must get past the resentment, guilt, and shame; you must let go of it. The way to let go is to forgive.

You must become willing to forgive those who harmed you, and you must also become willing to forgive yourself for the harm you have done to others. To forgive others and yourself will have the same effect on you it had on Bill. It will release your guilt and shame; it will release your resentment. These are things that have kept you stuck. This is not a simple task; it is an ongoing process. In Chapter 16 you will learn more about forgiveness.

◆ **EXERCISE 1** Think of some of your harmful actions. What harmful actions have you blamed on others?

_____

_____

_____

_____

_____

_____

_____

◆ **EXERCISE 2** How were those harmful actions really your responsibility? Do you accept responsibility?

_____

_____

_____

_____

_____

_____

◆ **EXERCISE 3** What harmful behaviors do you need to stop?

_____

_____

_____

_____

_____

_____

◆ **EXERCISE 4** Describe something you have done that you feel guilt or shame about. What can you do to release yourself from the guilt and shame?

_____

_____

_____

_____

_____

_____

◆ **EXERCISE 5** Make a list of people who hurt you. Do you have resentment toward them?

_____

_____

_____

_____

_____

◆ **EXERCISE 6** How could forgiving the people named above help your recovery?

_____

_____

_____

_____

_____

◆ **EXERCISE 7** Make a list of some of the things you need to forgive yourself for.

_____

_____

_____

_____

_____

You must realize you are never justified in using violence,
unless your life or the life of a loved one is in jeopardy.

LESSON 3

You used physical and verbal violence in the past to feel powerful. You used your angry behavior to gain power and control over other people, to control situations and things. You could always find an excuse to justify your violent behavior. You often felt the victims of your violence deserved what they got.

In truth, there were times when people treated you badly. They were rude to you, said things that hurt your feelings, and sometimes even hurt your body. You responded with anger and rage. You probably called it "getting even." You may have said, "Vengeance is sweet!" But where does it end? As someone with an anger problem, you must find other ways to respond when people hurt you. Revenge is a luxury you cannot afford.

You have an anger habit, if not a full-blown addiction to anger. You get drunk on anger and rage, you harm others, and then you pay dues. You lose something. You must ask yourself the same question Pathways to Peace founder Bill asked himself: "As someone with an anger problem, can I ever justify violence?"

You must put all arguments aside. Some people may think violence is justified. Maybe they can afford to think so. But in good conscience, you cannot. Not as a person who has an anger habit. You must commit yourself to the belief that violence in any form is never justified, unless, of course, your life or the life of a loved one is in danger.

◆ **EXERCISE 1** List two times you used physical or verbal violence to feel powerful.

_____

_____

◆ **EXERCISE 2** List two times you felt justified in using violence to control people, situations, and things.

_____

_____

◆ **EXERCISE 3** List two times you hurt people and felt your victims deserved it.

_____

_____

◆ **EXERCISE 4** Why, in nearly all cases, is violence never justified for you? What is the only time you would be justified in using violence?

_____

_____

_____

_____

_____

_____

_____

_____

_____

_____

_____

_____

_____

_____

_____

_____

You must learn ways to feel personal power without violating other people's right to feel safe in their person and property.

LESSON 4

Like Pathways to Peace founder Bill, you learned that anger made you feel powerful. You probably learned it at an early age, but now you have decided to change. Your angry behavior has harmed others and has harmed property. You have decided to stop using intimidation and violence as tools of power and control. To succeed, you must learn new skills, new ways to change how you feel. Throughout the rest of this workbook you will learn new ways to feel powerful.

◆ **EXERCISE 1** Think about your story. How old were you when you learned that anger made you feel powerful?

_____

◆ **EXERCISE 2** How would learning new ways to feel powerful help you?

_____

_____

_____

_____

_____

_____

_____

_____

_____

*You must treat all people and their property with the respect
and dignity that you, yourself, deserve and expect.*

LESSON 5

Like Bill, you may have been harmed by others. They may have injured your body and mind
and your respect and dignity. You may have felt worthless. You may have used anger and rage
to make others feel worthless, too. You may have robbed others of respect and dignity, the
way it had been taken from you. But now you see the people you hurt didn't deserve the pain
you caused them, and now you want to change. So you must promise yourself you will treat
others with respect and dignity—no matter what has been done to you, no matter how others may have hurt you.

◆ **EXERCISE 1** Describe an incident when someone robbed you of your respect and dignity.

_____

_____

_____

_____

_____

◆ **EXERCISE 2** Describe a way you robbed someone else of their respect and dignity.

_____

_____

_____

_____

◆ **EXERCISE 3** Are you now committed to treating others with respect and dignity?

_____

*You must let go of negative beliefs and adopt positive beliefs
about yourself, other people, and the world.*

LESSON 6

You have many negative beliefs that limit you. You must identify the ones that have kept you stuck, and let go of them. Then you must adopt new beliefs that will help you change your angry behavior. You will learn more about beliefs in Chapter 13.

◆ **EXERCISE** Identify one belief you have about yourself that keeps you stuck in your anger.

_____

_____

_____

_____

_____

_____

_____

_____

_____

_____

_____

_____

You must come to believe you can change and grow,
and that you have a special purpose to fulfill.

LESSON 7

You can change and grow. You may not believe that now, but you must come to believe it. In order to recover and heal from your anger habit, you must let go of the belief that you aren't capable of changing and growing.

Your life has a purpose. You may not believe that now, but you must try to come to believe it. The belief that your life has a purpose is one of the keys to personal change and growth; in fact, it could be the master key. If you believe you have a purpose, you will have a reason to change—a big reason—and you will have hope. You have a *big change* to make, and you must have a *big reason* to make the change.

◆ **EXERCISE 1** You may still believe you cannot change and grow. What will happen if you do not change this belief?

_____

_____

_____

_____

_____

◆ **EXERCISE 2** You may still believe your life has no meaning. How will that belief keep you stuck?

_____

_____

_____

_____

_____

You must continue your path of emotional, mental, and spiritual growth. You must forgive others and yourself. You must pass on what you are learning and help other angry people recover.

LESSON 8

Recovery is an ongoing process. You must continue your personal program of emotional, mental, and spiritual growth. If you continue to work hard, positive changes will happen. Your behavior will change. Your attitude will change. Your outlook will change. Your character will change in a major way. Having found your pathway to peace, you will experience the joy of helping others recover from their anger problem. You will be *transformed*.

◆ **EXERCISE 1** Why must you keep working hard at your recovery?

_____

_____

_____

_____

_____

◆ **EXERCISE 2** What will your rewards be if you continue to work hard?

_____

_____

_____

_____

◆ **EXERCISE 3** What does passing on what you are learning have to do with your personal growth?

_____

_____

_____

_____

_____

_____

_____

_____

_____

_____

_____

_____

_____

A Message from Bill

If I hadn't followed these steps, my recovery would never have begun.
They were the steps I took, but at first I was not aware that I was taking them.
Later I noticed my behavior was changing. I noticed that I was feeling better
about myself, other people, and the world. I knew, vaguely, that I was following some kind of plan. But I wanted to know exactly what I was doing. Then I
could help others. So I thought about it and then wrote it down.

5

Motivate Yourself to Change

Chapter 4 introduced you to the eight steps that are involved in recovering from your anger problem. Now that you have some idea of what is involved in the recovery process, you must get started along the recovery road. This chapter will help you motivate yourself to get on the road and stay on the road.

In this chapter you will learn a method that will increase your desire to stop using violence and increase your desire to recover from your anger habit. The motivation method you will learn is based on the story *A Christmas Carol* by Charles Dickens. You may have seen the movie or video, or you may have read the book. The main character is Ebenezer Scrooge.

You may recall that Scrooge was visited by several spirits. One of the spirits took Scrooge back into the past. That spirit showed Scrooge things he had said and done in the past that had harmed others, and it showed him things that he had lost because of his behavior.

Another spirit took Scrooge into the future. This spirit showed Scrooge how he would continue to hurt others if he didn't change, and it showed him what other things he would lose if he didn't change how he behaved.

A Message from Bill

Dickens was one of my favorite authors. His story *A Christmas Carol* always moved me. I read the book and watched the video many times over the years. I rewrote some of the story in order to suit my purpose, then used the story to increase my desire to stop using violent behavior. I followed my script pretty closely. I got good results. I wasn't too happy with how it made me feel at first, but it increased my desire to change; that's the result I was after. I read the script again whenever I feel my motivation to change start to weaken.

The spirits showed Scrooge he would have to change completely. They showed him he would have to change not only his behavior, but his entire character. The spirits showed Scrooge he would have to undergo a complete transformation. Otherwise, he would continue to lose things and never be happy. The lesson Scrooge learned from the spirits was a painful one, but the lesson also held a light of hope.

Scrooge's experience is the basis for the method you're about to learn. The method is written in the form of a script. You could simply read the script to yourself, but it would be better to have a friend read it to you while you sit back and listen. If you wish, you could have a counselor read it to you.

You need to have a good place in which to read the script, or have it read to you. Choose a quiet, comfortable place. Choose a place where you will not be disturbed for at least twenty minutes.

The script should be read slowly, with the reader pausing after each sentence. The pauses will allow you time to process and personalize the information. The script should be followed as it is written and should be read with feeling. The reading should take at least fifteen minutes. Anything less than fifteen minutes will not allow you to thoroughly process your feelings.

LESSON 1 ~ The Motivation Script

Part One

Close your eyes and relax, and think about your anger. Think about the things you have lost because of your anger habit. Think about the relationships you have lost. Think about how much self-respect you have lost. Think about how much money your anger and rage have cost you. Think about the effect anger and rage have had on your health. Notice how it has affected your ability to set and reach goals. Notice how it has affected your freedom. Get in touch with the feelings of guilt and shame anger has caused in your life. Become aware of the pain your anger and rage has caused others.

Now go back in your imagination to the first loss you suffered because of your anger. What was that first loss? Did someone you loved walk out of your life? Did you lose a friend? Did you lose your self-respect? Was that your first loss? Did you go to jail and lose your freedom? How did that first loss, whatever it was, make you feel? Did you feel proud of yourself? Or did you feel ashamed?

Now think of all the other things you lost because of your anger. Start with that first loss, and then think of the other things you lost from that first loss, right up to the present. Think about all of the losses, one by one. Take your time. Get in touch with how those losses made you feel; get in touch with the pain. People talked about Scrooge behind his back. They said negative things about him. What do you think people were saying about you behind your back?

Now like Scrooge, travel into the future. Go five years into the future, and imagine you are still using anger and rage to change how you feel. Carry all the pain of your past losses with you into the future. They're heavy, aren't they? They weigh you down, and every new loss adds weight to the load. Five more years have passed; you are still using anger like a drug to change how you feel. How many relationships have you lost now? How many friends have you lost? How many months have you spent in jail? Or how many years? What is your health like now? What do you think people are saying about you now behind your back? How much worse are things going for you now, with the passing of time?

Now jump ahead five more years. Ten years have gone by, and you are still using anger like a drug. What is your life like now? What has anger and rage cost you? How much freedom have you lost? Are you in prison now (or again)? Have you killed somebody in a fit of rage? Maybe someone has killed you, in self-defense! Have you lost all your friends? Is your self-respect totally gone? Do you even have a relationship anymore? Or are you living alone in a cardboard box under a bridge somewhere? What do you think people are saying about you behind your back now? You have been using anger and rage like a drug for ten more years. Have you also become addicted to alcohol or other drugs? Or have you relapsed back into drug use after some clean time? Maybe you have died of an overdose. Maybe they found your body in an alley somewhere, behind some garbage cans! How many people have you hurt? You have used anger to feel powerful for ten more years. Now how do you feel about yourself? Count up your losses. Get in touch with the pain.

(Pause here for at least sixty seconds.)

Part Two

In your imagination come back to the present. You can open your eyes while you rest for a few moments; like Scrooge, take a breather.

Now close your eyes again and prepare for another visit to the future. In your imagination, see yourself five years in the future. But this time you have stopped using anger like a drug to change how you feel. You have not committed a violent act for five whole years! You have stopped hurting people with words and actions; you have stopped breaking things; you have stopped threatening people. You aren't perfect—nobody is. You still get angry once in a while. After all, you're human! But you have stopped doing the things you used to do. You have learned how to manage your anger. You have stopped the violence and have learned new ways to respond to old triggers. You have been working a recovery program for five years.

You have been rage-free for five years; get in touch with the benefits! What is your life like now? What have you gained by changing your behavior? How have you benefitted from working a recovery program for five years? What are your relationships like? How have you benefitted financially? How has your health benefitted? And what about your self-respect? How do you feel about yourself now? Because you have been rage-free for five years, what have you been able to accomplish? What do you think people are saying about you now?

Now go five more years into the future. Carry all the benefits with you. Get in touch with how you will feel about yourself because you have changed. In your imagination, listen to the good things people will be saying about you. See yourself happy and loved. See yourself at peace, at last, with yourself and the world.

(Pause here for sixty seconds.)

Now come back to the present again, and make a choice. Choose the kind of future you want for yourself. Choose right now; you don't have any more time!

Now sit quietly and allow your mind to process what you have just done. Allow your mind to process the thoughts and memories; allow your body to process the feelings attached to the thoughts and memories. Spend at least five minutes processing.

You will want to use this method more than once. Repeat the method any time you notice a decrease in your motivation to change your behavior and recover from your anger habit.

◆ **EXERCISE 1** How did you feel after you finished Part One of the motivation script?

_____

_____

_____

_____

◆ **EXERCISE 2** How did you feel after you finished Part Two of the motivation script?

_____

_____

_____

_____

◆ **EXERCISE 3** What was the choice you made at the end of Part Two?

_____

_____

_____

_____

◆ **EXERCISE 4** What do you think about that choice now?

_____

_____

_____

_____

_____

_____

◆ **EXERCISE 5** Go back and read the script again. You can just read it to yourself this time. The script asks you to remember the first thing you lost because of anger. Write down what it was you lost.

_____

_____

_____

_____

_____

◆ **EXERCISE 6** Write down some of the other things you lost.

_____

_____

_____

_____

_____

◆ **EXERCISE 7** People said negative things about Scrooge behind his back. Write down what you think people were saying about you behind your back.

_____

_____

_____

_____

◆ **EXERCISE 8** Write down what you think you will lose in the future if you do not recover from your anger habit.

_____

_____

_____

_____

◆ **EXERCISE 9** You are now working a recovery program for your anger habit. You are learning how to change your behavior; you are learning how to stop using verbal abuse and violence. Write down how you think you will benefit if you continue your recovery.

_____

_____

_____

_____

_____

◆ **EXERCISE 10** What kinds of things would you like people to say about you?

_____

_____

_____

_____

_____

_____

_____

_____

6

Understand the Anger Process Using the Niagara Falls Metaphor

In Chapter 5, you learned an effective way to motivate yourself to continue the recovery process. In this chapter, you will learn another important concept that will enable you to more effectively track your progress.

A metaphor is a comparison. The Niagara Falls metaphor compares anger and rage to the Niagara River and the Niagara Falls.

LESSON 1 ~ A Little Bit About the Niagara Falls

Practically everyone knows about the Niagara River and the Niagara Falls. People from all over the world have visited the Falls. If you have not visited it, you have seen it in movies. It is one of the Seven Wonders of the World, one of the most awesome natural sights a human being could ever see.

The power of the Falls is almost beyond belief. The volume of water that goes over the Falls also stretches the imagination—water pours over the Falls at the rate of 203,000 gallons per second! But just a few miles upstream from the Falls, the river moves slowly in its channel. You can't see or hear the Falls from there and people safely fish from boats in that part of the river. Of course, boats have an engine and a pair of oars, so if you were in a boat in this calm section of the river, you would have some control over your boat.

But what would happen if your engine failed and you lost your oars overboard? You would be in deep trouble! You would no longer have control over your boat and would be at the mercy of the current! The current would carry you toward the Falls at an ever-increasing rate of speed. The Niagara River moves faster and faster the closer it gets to the Falls. The power and tension of the river increases.

If you yelled for help at that point, someone might hear you and respond; you could be saved from going over the Falls. Another boat could reach you and tow you and your boat to shore, or a helicopter could drop a line and pluck you out of the river.

But a hundred yards or so from the brink of the Falls, the river becomes a rushing torrent. If you weren't saved before you got to that point, all would be lost. No one could overcome the power of the river at that point. In order to avoid injury or death you have to find a way to get out of the river before then. That part of the Niagara River is called *the point of no return.*

People who fish in the Niagara River come prepared. Few people lose control and plunge to their death. Accidents happen sometimes, but they are rare. Of course, some people have actually chosen to take the plunge over the Falls for glory and fame. They used all kinds of ways, even wrapping themselves in rubber tires. But it is a 160-foot plunge to the bottom of the gorge. Hitting water from that height is like diving from the top of an eight-story building onto concrete. And the bottom of the gorge is littered with boulders; you can count on the fingers of one hand the number of people who have survived a plunge over the Falls. A few people have even used the Falls to commit suicide.

◆ **EXERCISE 1** Probably you have seen pictures of the Niagara Falls. You may even have seen it in person. Close your eyes and picture the Niagara Falls in your mind. Describe how your picture of the Niagara Falls connects with your anger.

_____

_____

_____

_____

◆ **EXERCISE 2** When you think of the Niagara Falls, what do you find interesting about it?

_____

_____

_____

_____

THE NIAGARA FALLS METAPHOR

The Anger Process

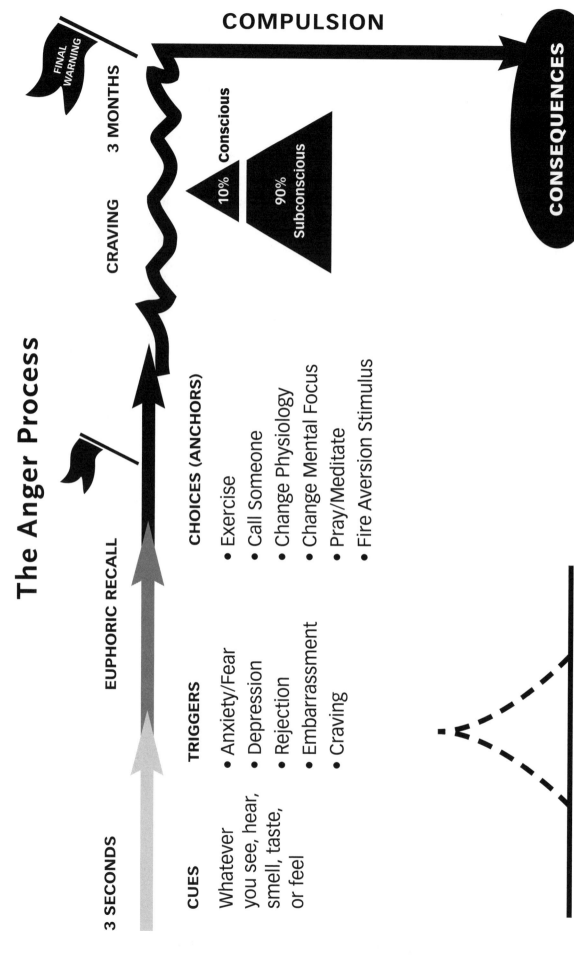

COMPULSION

FINAL WARNING

3 MONTHS

CRAVING

10% **Conscious**

90% **Subconscious**

CONSEQUENCES

EUPHORIC RECALL

3 SECONDS

CUES

Whatever you see, hear, smell, taste, or feel

TRIGGERS

• Anxiety/Fear
• Depression
• Rejection
• Embarrassment
• Craving

CHOICES (ANCHORS)

• Exercise
• Call Someone
• Change Physiology
• Change Mental Focus
• Pray/Meditate
• Fire Aversion Stimulus

NORMAL BASELINE TENSION

According to the Niagara Falls metaphor, when you are angry it is like ending up in a small boat in the Niagara River, except that your boat is without engine and oars. Go back and read about the Niagara Falls again, but this time think about your anger as you read. Imagine that the process of getting angry is like the process of losing control of your boat and being swept closer and closer to the brink of the falls. It's a scary image, isn't it? But it's one that will help you understand what happens inside when you begin to get angry.

When you get angry, you do things that you regret. You hurt people, animals, or things, or you say things that you later regret. You become verbally abusive or physically violent. When you are abusive or violent, that is like going over the Niagara Falls. Someone or something gets hurt, and then you pay consequences. You lose something you value, such as friends or relationships or your freedom.

Also, you are not aware of being in the river. That's another part of the metaphor. That's a scary thought, but it is true. You use anger like a drug and have developed an anger habit. You may, in fact, have developed an addiction to anger. When you have a habit or are addicted to something, you are often not aware of the behavior connected with your habit or addiction. You are not aware when you are in the process of the habit or addiction. In this chapter you will learn how to be aware when you are in the process called anger and rage. In the next chapter you will learn how to stop the process and get out of the river.

◆ **EXERCISE 1** How is getting angry like being in the Niagara River?

_____

_____

_____

_____

◆ **EXERCISE 2** Part of the metaphor talks about "going over the falls." When you think about your anger, what does it mean to "go over the falls"?

_____

_____

_____

_____

STAGE 1 | *Cues and Triggers (Feelings)—Plunging into the River*

"Cues" can be people, places, and things. Cues are things you can see or hear. A person you see on the street could be a cue or the sound of a person's voice could be a cue. Some cues are things you remember. The memory of a person's face could be a cue. The memory of a person's voice or the words they said could be a cue. Sometimes you can avoid cues, but most of the time you will have little control over cues that happen. It is the "stuff of life" that happens and is often beyond your control. The good news is that you can *learn* how to control memory cues and you can *learn* how to deal with cues you cannot avoid. The key word is *learn*.

Cues connect to feelings, both good ones and bad ones. Bad feelings are negative; good feelings are positive. Whether a cue leads to a bad feeling or a good one depends on how you think about the cue. If you think of the cue as painful, it will cause a bad feeling. If you think of the cue as pleasurable, it will cause a good feeling. ***The bad feelings, caused by cues, are the triggers for anger and rage.***

Cues are happening all the time. When a cue is painful, it leads to a bad feeling, and then the bad feeling becomes an anger trigger. Anger is always triggered by bad feelings, not by good ones. Feelings like fear or frustration are typical anger triggers. These bad feelings cause your tension level to increase from its normal, or "baseline" level, to a higher than normal tension level. The increased tension is what causes you to end up in the anger process. To use the metaphor (see page 84), it is what causes you to end up in the Niagara River in a small boat without engine or oars. Painful feelings are triggers that plunge you into the river.

As soon as you become aware of a trigger, you should think: *"I have only three seconds to get out of here!"* If you assume you have only three seconds to get out of the anger process, you may have a chance to interrupt the process before it's too late—before you reach the point of no return and plunge over the Falls.

A key to recovery from an anger habit is to learn how to manage the bad feelings that trigger your anger; then you need to back up even farther to learn how to deal with cues that initially cause the bad feelings. You will learn how to deal with cues that cause bad feelings in the next chapter.

◆ **EXERCISE 1** Name three people, places, and things that you think are cues that lead to your anger triggers.

_____

_____

_____

◆ **EXERCISE 2** Name the trigger (bad feeling) that each cue connects to.

_____

_____

_____

_____

_____

◆ **EXERCISE 3** What is the difference between a cue and a trigger? Give two examples of each.

_____

_____

_____

_____

_____

_____

STAGE 2 | *Euphoric Recall (First Red Flag)*

Euphoric means pleasurable; *recall* means to remember. *Euphoric recall* is a memory of a time when you used anger and it made you feel good; it made you feel high and you didn't suffer bad consequences. You didn't go to jail, you didn't get hurt or hurt someone you loved. You didn't end up suffering some kind of punishment. Instead, you felt rewarded. You felt powerful. Euphoric recall is a natural part of the anger process.

You are already in the Niagara River before euphoric recall happens (see page 84). Whenever you experience euphoric recall, you are heading toward the Falls. It also means your tension level has risen even higher. Your tension level automatically increases when you don't do something right away to interrupt an anger trigger. Your increased tension causes euphoric recall.

You have no control over euphoric recall; it happens automatically. You are not consciously aware when it happens, but euphoric recall causes you to move faster toward the

Falls. When you experience euphoric recall, you begin to anticipate the pleasure you will feel when you act out in anger. The Niagara River acts much like the anger process. The closer the Niagara River gets to the Falls, the more the tension and speed of the river increases. During euphoric recall, your brain remembers a time when you used anger and you experienced pleasurable results; you felt powerful and you avoided negative results. The anticipation of pleasure, along with the increased tension, accelerates your desire to use anger and violence. It pushes you faster and faster toward the point of no return.

You must learn to see euphoric recall as a big red warning flag. As a warning flag, euphoric recall pops up out of the river and loudly says, "You fool! You are in the Niagara River, heading for the Falls!"

◆ **EXERCISE 1** What does *euphoric recall* mean?

_____

_____

_____

◆ **EXERCISE 2** Why is euphoric recall called a "red flag"?

_____

_____

_____

STAGE 3 | *Craving (Final Warning Flag)*

A craving is a strong urge. In this case, a craving is a strong urge to act out your anger.

Think back on the Niagara Falls metaphor illustrated on page 84. Metaphorically speaking, the Niagara River is a process that never stops and never slows down. What happens to the Niagara River the closer it gets to the Falls? You have already learned the answer to this question: The tension and speed of the river increases. The anger process doesn't stop or slow down either—your tension keeps increasing, like the river. You move faster and closer to angry behavior. You must do something to interrupt the process.

When you have a craving to use anger, you are close—very close—to the Falls. The river has picked up speed, meaning your tension level has increased again. *The increase in your tension level causes the craving.*

It is much harder to fight off the craving than to fight off euphoric recall; that is why it is so important to get out of the river as soon as possible. The closer you get to the Falls, the harder it is to get out.

A craving is a bigger, brighter red flag. It says, "You fool! Not only are you in the Niagara River heading for the Falls, you are right at the brink! You are in white water!" This is the final warning flag!

During the craving stage, it is as though two voices start arguing inside your head; it is as though two different people are inside your head yelling at each other. You may not be consciously aware of them, but they are there. One voice urges you to do or say something violent. It says, "Do it! Do something violent!" That voice takes you into deep denial and it wants you to justify and rationalize. That voice doesn't want you to remember the consequences you experienced when you used anger and rage in the past. It wants you to forget about that and think only of the pleasure you might experience. The other voice urges you not to be violent. It says, "No. Don't!" That voice wants you to avoid violence. It wants you to stop and think. It wants you to remember the negative consequences you suffered; that voice wants you to remember the guilt and remorse you felt because of the pain you caused others. You struggle with trying to decide which voice to listen to. But by the time you experience a craving to use anger, your tension level is extremely high. You will have to make a decision very quickly, because you are close to the point of no return. You must not give in to the first voice; if you listen to the first voice, you lose.

◆ **EXERCISE 1** Stage Three of the anger process is called a *craving*. What does the word *craving* mean?

_____

_____

_____

_____

_____

◆ **EXERCISE 2** How is a craving different from euphoric recall?

_____

_____

_____

_____

_____

◆ **EXERCISE 3** Why is a craving called the "final warning flag"? Where are you in the river when a craving happens?

_____

_____

_____

_____

_____

STAGE 4 | _Compulsion_

Up to this point you have had a choice. You had opportunities to stop yourself from going over the Falls (see page 84). You had opportunities to interrupt the process because you were _consciously aware_ you were in the river, and you had two strong warnings that danger lay ahead.

But there is a big difference between a _craving_ and a _compulsion_. When you felt a craving, you still had a choice. As stated on the previous page, you were still consciously aware you were in the river.

> ### _When you feel a compulsion to do anything,_
> ### _whatever it may be, you no longer have a choice._

When you have a _compulsion_ to use anger, you no longer have a choice. You have no choice because you are no longer aware you are in the river. When you feel a compulsion, it means you can't stop; it means you are already over the Falls. It means your tension has increased beyond the point of no return. It means you have lost control. When you feel a compulsion to use anger to change how you feel, to change a feeling of powerlessness into a feeling of power, you no longer have control. The anger process has taken control of you.

Here is another way to understand a compulsion. The mind is like an iceberg. An iceberg sits low in the water. Only about 10 percent of the iceberg—just the tip—shows above the water line; the other 90 percent floats under water, hidden from view. The 10 percent that rides above the water line represents the _conscious mind._ The part under water represents the _subconscious mind._ When you feel a compulsion, your conscious mind stops functioning and your subconscious mind takes over. That's when you lose control. You end up going over the Falls, unable to stop yourself. Then you crash at the bottom of the gorge and have negative results.

Your anger is a habit. You have many other habits besides your anger habit; all are stored in your subconscious mind. Habits are automatic behaviors. Your habits stay down in the subconscious mind until something triggers them into action. It is as though they are asleep there. Things that wake up habits are called triggers (feelings). Every habit has its own trigger or triggers.

Your subconscious mind watches for triggers. When a trigger connected to a certain habit occurs, the subconscious mind notices it, and then it wakes up the habit that was asleep in your subconscious mind and causes you to go into action—*automatically.*

◆ **EXERCISE 1** What does it mean to have a *compulsion?*

_____

_____

_____

_____

◆ **EXERCISE 2** Why do you no longer have a choice once you reach the compulsion stage?

_____

_____

_____

_____

◆ **EXERCISE 3** When you reach the compulsion stage, who or what is in control of the anger process?

_____

_____

_____

_____

STAGE 5 | *Consequences (Negative Results)*

You suffer consequences when you use anger and rage to change how you feel. *Consequences* are negative results. Losing something you value is a negative result. When you go over the Falls (see the metaphor illustrated on page 84), you cannot avoid losing something you value. You may get arrested and lose your freedom. You may lose an opportunity, or your spouse, or your self-respect. Of course, you end up feeling bad instead of good. You end up feeling guilty and ashamed, or embarrassed. The point is, you have to pay consequences.

The guilt, shame, and embarrassment become triggers, too. These bad feelings keep you stuck in the process; they send you right back into the river. The process becomes a circulating pump: A cue happens. That is, you see or hear or remember something that leads to a bad feeling. The bad feeling triggers your anger; you plunge into the river and harm someone or something; you go over the falls and crash down into the rocky gorge; you lose something you value and then you feel guilty and ashamed; then the guilt and shame circulates you back through the process. Pretty soon you think you must be crazy.

But there is a way out. You can learn how to stop the madness once and for all and get out of the dangerous Niagara River. You can change. The next chapter will help you learn how.

◆ **EXERCISE 1** What are *consequences?*

_____

_____

_____

_____

A Message from Julio

I'm Julio. I live in Texas and I've got a big anger problem. I have to be honest. I don't just have an anger habit; I'm addicted to anger.

I've never been to the Niagara Falls, but I know about rivers and I know about waterfalls. I've lived near the Rio Grande River ever since I moved here from Mexico with my father and mother, when I was five years old. Comparing anger to the Niagara Falls helps me understand my anger problem better than anything else. It helps me know when I'm in the anger process, and it helps me know where I am in the process and what I need to do to get out. I use the Niagara Falls metaphor to help me stay aware of the anger process. I can say to myself, "I'm starting to get angry. I'm in the river. What part am I in? What do I need to do to get out?"

◆ **EXERCISE 2** Write down three consequences you have had because of your anger.

_____

_____

_____

◆ **EXERCISE 3** Describe the "circulating pump" effect of guilt and shame.

_____

_____

_____

_____

◆ **EXERCISE 4** Name the five stages of the anger process.

_____

_____

_____

_____

7

Interrupt the Process

In Chapter 6 you learned how to use the Niagara Falls metaphor, which compares anger to a trip down the Niagara River and over the Falls, to increase your understanding of how the anger process works. In this chapter you will learn how to interrupt the anger process and save yourself from going over the Falls.

You learned your anger habit by repeating angry behavior over and over in response to certain feelings (triggers). Your anger became a habit, an automatic behavior. Your anger habit is an automatic behavior that is now permanently stored in your subconscious mind, along with all your other habits.

Now that your angry behavior has become a habit, you respond automatically with anger whenever your brain notices one of your anger triggers. Your subconscious mind has taken over the operation of your anger habit, so you have lost control of the process. Now you find yourself doing or saying angry things even when you don't want to.

But you can learn new ways to respond to the same old triggers. You can learn new behaviors and you can decide to make different choices. Then you can learn to repeat the new behaviors over and over in response to triggers. Learning new behaviors, and then learning how to repeat the new behaviors instead of old angry behaviors when triggers occur, is the beginning of recovery from your anger habit. It is the beginning of the healing process. Finally, the new behaviors will grow into a new habit and become automatic. *You will acquire a new habit called recovery,* and then your subconscious mind will take over the operation of the healing process.

LESSON 1 ~ Will You Ever Forget Your Anger Habit?

You will never forget your anger habit. Once a behavior becomes a habit, your brain *cannot* forget it. Habits are stored in brain cells and in brain tissue. So you will never forget how to use anger and violence to change how you feel.

Consider the skills for driving a car. Your driving skills are a habit. Your driving skills are stored in your subconscious mind. Will you ever forget how to drive a car? No. You will never forget how to drive a car, and you will never forget how to use anger to change how you feel.

A Message from David

My name is David. I'm from New York.

I was working a good anger recovery program. I learned some new skills, and I was handling triggers better than ever. I hadn't had an outburst in three months; then I got a little complacent. I stopped focusing on my program as much. I stopped doing some of the things that I had learned. I wish I hadn't. I started to think I had it made, that I didn't have to think about my recovery anymore. I forgot that I had an anger habit. About two weeks later, somebody said something—it doesn't matter what. What the person said caused me to feel embarrassed, and embarrassment is one of my major triggers. I plunged into the river. Before I knew it, I was too far downstream. I went off on the person. He was my boss. I didn't physically attack him or break anything. It was all verbal: I shouted and swore. Bottom line is, I lost my job. Man, I needed that job! I found out I hadn't forgotten how to use anger to change how I felt.

(*Note:* There is one way to forget your anger habit, but it would be a drastic measure. You could have a brain surgeon remove the *tissue* in the part of your brain where your anger habit is stored. That is the only way you can forget any habit.)

You are a human being. You will end up in the anger process from time to time no matter how hard you try to avoid it. But you can learn how to get out of the river before you go over the Falls. You can also choose to stay in the process. If you choose to stay in the process even though you now know how it works, then your tension will continue to increase. Finally your old anger habit will take control again. You will feel a compulsion, and your anger habit will escape from your subconscious mind like a raging beast from its cage. You will plunge over the Falls again, because you will no longer have a choice.

◆ **EXERCISE** Why will you never be able to forget your anger habit?

_____

_____

_____

_____

_____

_____

STEP 1 | *Check Your Body*

You are not consciously aware when your anger habit gets triggered. A trigger occurs, but you don't notice it. That is because your subconscious mind operates your anger habit. Your subconscious mind notices the trigger, but it doesn't let your conscious mind know. So *you* are not aware of the trigger.

Remember the metaphor? Addictive anger is like the Niagara River and the Niagara Falls. If you are not aware you are in the river, you will not be able to get out in time and you will go over the Falls. You must learn to be aware when you are in the river. You must learn to be aware you are in the river as soon as a trigger occurs. The trigger is the first step of your anger habit; it is what plunges you into the river. So the first step to getting out of the river is knowing you are in it.

Remember the term *baseline tension?* If you are alive, you already have a certain level of tension in your body, called baseline tension. That is your normal tension level. When an anger trigger occurs, your tension level suddenly increases. It shoots up above normal: It *spikes.* You have no conscious control over the increased tension. It is like what happens when you sit down and cross your legs and tap that certain spot under your kneecap. When you tap that spot, your lower leg automatically jumps. It is sometimes called the *knee-jerk* response. It is a *reflex.* When an anger trigger occurs, your tension level responds in a similar way. It jumps higher.

Your body knows immediately when an anger trigger occurs. It immediately sends you the message that your tension level has increased. But you must learn to get in touch with how your body sends you the message. Your tension will increase more in a certain body area than in another—every body sends the message in a unique way. That is, not everyone feels the increased tension in the same body area. First, you must find out *where* you feel the increased tension in your body, and then you must learn to notice *when* the tension level in that body area increases. Then you will have a handy way to know when you are in the anger process. The trigger causing the increased tension could be fear or frustration; it could be anxiety or disappointment. The trigger could be any one of a thousand negative feelings, but you don't have to know what the trigger is. All you have to know is that your tension level has increased.

Step One in interrupting the anger habit is to check your body. Check to discover where your body feels increased tension; then you will be able to notice when you are in the anger process. The exercise below will help you learn where you feel increased tension in your body.

◆ **EXERCISE**

    A. Think of a time you were angry.

    B. While you are thinking about it, pay attention to your body tension right now.

    C. Notice exactly where your body feels the most tension.

When an anger trigger happens, I feel a sudden increase in tension in my (circle the body area that applies to you): stomach, lower back, back of the neck, jaws, behind my eyes, other (write down the area).

_____

_____

_____

_____

_____

    Now you know what body area you feel increased tension in when a trigger happens. Now you have a way of knowing when you are in the river. Practice paying attention to that area of your body. You must learn to notice anger triggers as soon as possible, so you will have the best possible chance of getting out of the river. If you do not notice the triggers right away, your risk increases. If you do not notice the triggers until you feel a compulsion, it will be too late, because by then you will already be over the Falls.

STEP 2 | *List Your Triggers, Choices, and Consequences, and List the Benefits of Changing Your Angry Behavior*

Step One in interrupting the anger process is to find a way to know you are in the process. You just learned to get in touch with how your body tells you when your tension increases. Now you must learn how to be consciously aware of the entire anger process. You must learn how to be consciously aware of what your triggers are; you must learn how to be consciously aware of your choices; and you must learn how to be consciously aware of your consequences (what you will lose if you go over the Niagara Falls again). You must also learn to be consciously aware of the benefits of recovering from your anger habit. Until you have learned how to maintain conscious awareness of the process, your anger habit will continue to control you and run your life. You must take back control.

    In Step Two, you must list your triggers, choices, and consequences, and you must list the benefits of changing your behavior. You made a short list of triggers and consequences in Chapter 6. Now it is time to expand that list, and it is time to list the benefits you will enjoy if you change your behavior. A special page has been provided at the end of this chapter to complete this lesson.

Important: After you have made your list, make three copies. Carry one copy of your list in your wallet or purse. Tape a copy of your list to the wall next to the bathroom mirror. Keep a copy of your list where you read or watch television. Look at the list every day. Looking at the list will help you stay consciously aware of how your anger habit works, and it will help you stay aware of how you will profit from changing the behavior. What will happen if you simply make the list and then never refer to it again? The answer is obvious: Once again you will forget how your anger habit works. Your anger habit will drop back down into the murky bottom layers of your subconscious mind; it will take charge of your life again. You will continue hurting others and yourself.

◆ Triggers

You have learned that anger triggers are always *negative feelings,* like those listed below. You know your triggers put the anger process in motion. Ask yourself: "What are the feelings that are the triggers for my anger and rage?"

Examples of Triggers

- embarrassment
- disappointment
- frustration
- anxiety

Each of these examples of triggers are common anger triggers; surely one or more of them apply to you. But there are probably many others that apply to you that are not listed among the examples above. Make sure you list all of your major triggers.

◆ Choices

Choices are things you could do instead of responding to anger triggers in the same old destructive way. Below is a brief list of possible choices. Whatever choices you choose to put on your list must be your choices, not someone else's choices. The choices you list must be things you would actually do. Also, you need a lot of choices. You need choices that will work any time, anywhere. You need choices that will work at two o'clock in the afternoon when you are at work; you need choices that will work at two o'clock in the morning when you are home and can't sleep. You need choices that will work no matter *when* you are in the river, and no matter *where* you are in the river. You may be way upstream where the river runs slowly or way downstream where the river runs faster, down closer to the point of no return.

When you list your choices, ask yourself: "What could I do instead of going over the Falls when a trigger occurs?"

Examples of choices

- call someone on the phone
- meditate
- exercise
- walk away
- pray

Later in the workbook you will learn other new choices. Be sure to add them to your list.

◆ Consequences

Going over the Falls means *acting out your anger*. Yelling, name-calling, hitting—these are examples of going over the Falls. Whenever you go over the Falls, other people suffer the consequences of your actions. Your actions hurt people physically, mentally, or emotionally; you cause them pain. When you act out in anger and hurt other people, you end up with consequences, too. You lose something you value. No one goes over the Niagara Falls without suffering consequences. The list of consequences below is just to get you started. When you make your list, get in touch with how you will feel if you suffer the losses on your list.

What do you think you might lose if you go over the Niagara Falls again? Will you end up in prison this time? Maybe for life, because you kill someone in a fit of rage? Will you lose that one human being who cares anything at all about you anymore? What will you lose? To get started, ask yourself this question: "What will I lose if I go over the Niagara Falls again?" Pay attention to how the losses make you feel.

Examples of Consequences

- loss of spouse
- loss of job
- loss of freedom
- loss of self-respect

◆ Benefits of Changing Your Angry Behavior

It is hard to change any behavior that has become a habit. You have learned you have an anger habit. Knowing what you will *lose* if you don't change your behavior is important, but knowing how you will *benefit* if you do change the behavior is also important. If you cannot see a benefit, it will be harder to change your behavior and harder to keep the behavior changed. To *benefit* means good things will happen for you. Ask yourself: "How will I benefit by stopping my angry behavior?"

Examples of Benefits

- more trust in relationships
- greater peace of mind
- potential to get a better job
- longer life
- increased personal freedom
- ability to keep a job
- better health

Making this list is an important part of your recovery from your anger habit; it is an important part of the healing process. Take your time when making your list.

How Your Anger Works and How You Will Profit from Changing Your Behavior

TRIGGERS	CHOICES	CONSEQUENCES	BENEFITS

Here's another important idea, another important part of the metaphor. Each new choice is like an anchor in the bottom of your boat. Each anchor has a different length of rope attached. When a trigger occurs, you must throw an anchor toward shore and hold on to the end of the rope. The anchor must sink into the earth on the other side of the river, and then *you* must pull yourself out of the river. Notice the key word: *YOU.*

Your new program will seem strange and uncomfortable to you at first. You may find some of your new choices don't work as well as you thought they would. If so, it is okay to change them or add new ones. The same is true of triggers, consequences, and benefits. Change and add to your list when you need to. Your recovery program, like you, is a work in progress! The secret to your success is to keep working on it.

Any program of recovery, whether from drug or alcohol addiction or from anger addiction, must be *self-initiated* and *self-maintained.* That means you have to be the one in charge. It means you have to be the one who decides and the one who acts. That is how recovery works.

Although you must not rely on someone else to save you, it is also extremely important to reach out for help. In fact, you should ask for help wherever and whenever possible. Attending Pathways to Peace meetings can provide the kind of help you need (you will learn more about Pathways to Peace at the end of this workbook). Talking with a counselor can help. Yet you must be in charge of your own recovery; you must take charge of the process. You are the one who is responsible for your healing. You run the show.

◆ **EXERCISE** Step Three to interrupt the anger process is the action step. What does it tell you to do?

_____

_____

_____

_____

_____

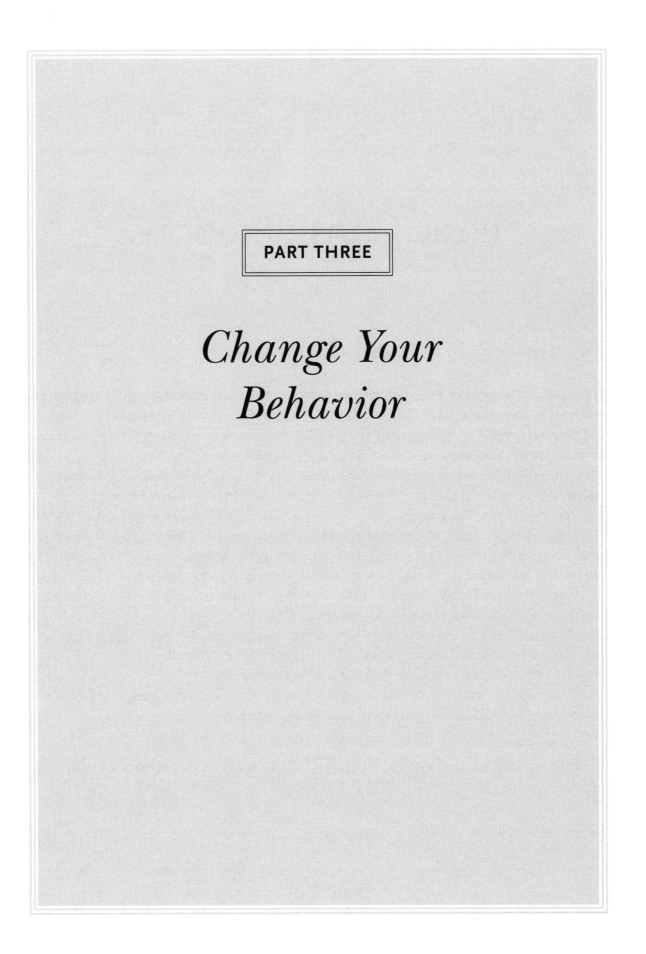

PART THREE

*Change Your
Behavior*

8

Basic Considerations

In Chapter 7 you learned a three-step method to interrupt the anger process. In this chapter, you will learn how important it is to pay attention to the basics of nutrition, sleep and rest, exercise, and personal scheduling. Also, you will learn a relaxation technique designed to help you deal more effectively with stress, one of the major triggers for anger.

How you take care of your body has a great deal to do with how you feel. Nutrition has a direct effect on the biological (physical) part of recovery from an anger habit.

Poor nutrition has a negative effect on your ability to manage anger. A diet high in sugar, for example, can lead to mood swings that may intensify anger triggers. You need a well-balanced diet that is low in sugar. You need plenty of protein. Ideally you should eat a variety of foods, including plenty of fresh fruits and vegetables. Try new fruits and vegetables; they add texture, color, and taste, and make a meal more interesting. They also add vitamins and make preparing and eating food more fun.

Use of caffeine increases your body's tension level and makes it harder to control your anger. Use of alcohol and other drugs also has a negative effect. You will learn more about the negative effects of alcohol and other drugs later in the workbook.

You need to have regular meals. Going long periods without eating a regular meal (more than five to six hours) makes you more sensitive to anger triggers.

◆ **EXERCISE** Pay attention to your diet over the course of a week. Is your diet well balanced with plenty of protein foods and not too much sugar?

_____

_____

LESSON 2 ~ Sleep and Rest

You would need adequate sleep and rest even if you didn't have an anger problem. As a person with an anger problem, you need to pay close attention to how much sleep and rest you get. Inadequate sleep and rest will intensify your anger triggers.

Establish regular bedtimes and regular wake-up times. Avoid sleeping during the day as a way to deal with boredom; it will make it harder to get the solid nighttime sleep your body needs. Once you have established good sleep patterns, you will feel more rested and you will be less likely to get angry.

◆ **EXERCISE** Do you get adequate sleep and rest? How do you feel when you get up in the morning? Do you feel rested? Or do you feel you need more sleep?

_____

_____

_____

_____

_____

_____

LESSON 3 ~ Physical Exercise

Your body needs exercise. Regular exercise releases "feel-good" chemicals, called endorphins, from your brain. These chemicals have a positive effect on your self-esteem. Regular exercise also gives you a sense of accomplishment.

You should exercise regularly, but you should not over-exercise. There are many kinds of exercise. For example, you could pump iron, or you could walk or jog.

Note: Check with your doctor before starting any exercise program.

◆ **EXERCISE 1** What kinds of exercise would you enjoy? (name three)

_____

_____

◆ **EXERCISE 2** How will you get one of these exercise programs going? When will you start?

_____

_____

_____

_____

_____

_____

LESSON 4 ~ Relaxation

Relaxation is another important basic consideration. You need to know how to relax in order to deal effectively with stress. Stress is a major anger trigger. In the past you used anger and violence to deal with stress, but now you must learn how to relax as a way to deal with stress. The relaxation method below will help you manage stress. It is an easy method that you can learn quickly and benefit from immediately.

A Message from George

I'm George, an anger addict from Racine, Wisconsin.

Sometimes I ate right, sometimes I didn't. I went years without a full night's sleep. I exercised too little or too much. I didn't know how to relax. In the past I used alcohol and other drugs in order to relax; that didn't work most of the time. In fact, sometimes the alcohol and drugs increased my stress level instead of lowering it. When that happened, it drove me crazy!

Then I stopped using alcohol and other drugs. I had to. Then I became aware of my anger habit, and I became aware of how my lousy eating habits and lack of exercise were affecting my mood. I read a book on nutrition and got started on a sensible exercise program. I stopped drinking coffee before going to bed. I exercised moderately. My mood improved and I slept better.

Later I saw how stress (frustration, anxiety, etc.) triggered my anger, so I knew I had to learn how to relax. I attended some relaxation classes. After a couple of weeks, I was able to relax more than I had ever been able to relax in the past. That also helped my sleep problem. Making these changes made it easier to deal with my anger.

◆ The Best Position to Use

The best position for relaxation is whatever works best for you. You need to find a comfortable position where you can sit for ten to twenty minutes without cramping or falling asleep. You could sit cross-legged on the floor, or you could sit in a chair. If you sit in a chair, sit up straight with your feet on the floor; that seems to works best for most people. Try different positions until you find one that works for you.

◆ The Best Place to Relax

As with the best position, the best place is wherever works for you. It should be a private space where you can be alone in silence. If one place doesn't work, choose another place.

◆ The Best Time to Relax

The best time of the day to relax is whatever time of the day or night suits you best.

◆ How to Relax

It's a good idea to record the meditation steps outlined below on audiotapes. Then you can sit back, relax, and listen to the instructions without worrying about leaving something out.

Relaxation is a learned process, a step-by-step procedure like driving a car or brushing your teeth. Go to your place of relaxation, and assume the position you decided to use when you relax. Turn the lights down. You may want to light a candle. Here are the steps:

1. Start by breathing slowly and deeply, and continue to breathe that way.

2. Relax your posture.

3. With your eyes open, and while continuing to breathe deeply and slowly, make three statements (silently, not aloud) about what you see. For example, "I see the room bathed in candlelight; I see a chair over in the corner; I see shadows dancing on the wall in the candlelight." Think the words on the out-breath.

    At the end of the third statement, add "and now I'm beginning to feel relaxed and calm." Now close your eyes and go to step four.

4. With your eyes closed now, and continuing to breathe deeply and slowly, think three statements about what you hear, thinking the words on the out-breath as before. For example, "I hear the sound of a dog barking in the distance; I hear the sound of water running in the kitchen; I hear the rhythmic sound of my own heartbeat; and now I'm beginning to feel more relaxed and calm."

    Switching from what you see to what you hear allows your conscious mind to let go of visual images so that it can concentrate on what you hear.

5. Continuing the same breathing pattern, with your eyes shut, make three statements about what you are feeling externally, thinking the words as you breathe

out. For example, "I can feel the pressure of my feet against the floor; I can feel the pressure of my back against the chair; I can feel the rise and fall of my chest as I breathe in and out; and now I feel calm and relaxed."

This step allows your mind to let go of auditory input (what you hear) so that it can focus on what you are feeling.

By now, you will have begun to relax. This method works by causing the mind to let go of the normal conscious state in a step-by-step fashion. One by one your senses (sight, hearing, and touch) disengage. Your heart rate slows down. Your blood pressure decreases. Your body becomes relaxed. Your mind shifts its focus inward.

With practice, you will be able to relax quickly using this method. Practice this relaxation method at least once a day. Twice a day would be better.

You could take a relaxation training class. Classes, which are usually not expensive, may help you learn to relax more quickly. Consult the phone directory yellow pages. Find out if there is an affordable relaxation class in your area.

◆ **EXERCISE** How did you feel after you tried the relaxation method described above?

_____

_____

_____

_____

_____

_____

_____

_____

_____

_____

_____

_____

LESSON 5 ~ Maintain a Schedule

In order to maintain an effective anger recovery program, you must maintain a schedule. You must schedule time for growth and development at each recovery level. You need to schedule time for all of the basics. You must schedule meal times, so that you do not skip meals or eat poor meals on the run. You must schedule time for sleep and rest. You must schedule time for exercise, and you must schedule time for relaxation.

Here is an example of a schedule format that covers the basic considerations:

DAILY SCHEDULE

	Breakfast	Lunch	Dinner	Exercise	Relaxation	Sleep
Time	7:00 A.M.	12:30 P.M.	6:00 P.M.	7:00 P.M.	10:00 P.M.	11:00 P.M.
Day	Daily	Daily	Daily	M, W, F	Daily	Daily

◆ **EXERCISE** Make a daily schedule that covers all four basic considerations. Use the form provided on the following page and keep in mind that multiple blank schedules have been included so you can make updates or revisions as needed.

Note: Build a little flexibility into your schedule; cut yourself some slack. There will be times when you can't stick to your schedule, but just do your best.

	Breakfast	Lunch	Dinner	Exercise	Relaxation	Sleep
Time						
Day						

	Breakfast	Lunch	Dinner	Exercise	Relaxation	Sleep
Time						
Day						

	Breakfast	Lunch	Dinner	Exercise	Relaxation	Sleep
Time						
Day						

	Breakfast	Lunch	Dinner	Exercise	Relaxation	Sleep
Time						
Day						

	Breakfast	Lunch	Dinner	Exercise	Relaxation	Sleep
Time						
Day						

9

Skills

In Chapter 8 you learned about the importance of paying attention to certain "basics" such as nutrition and rest. In this chapter you will learn some specific hands-on skills to help you stay out of the river and on the road to recovery.

Remember that in the Niagara Falls metaphor, you had anchors in your boat that you could use to pull yourself to safety? Think of skills as "anchors" in your boat. Skills are choices.

What you think about causes how you feel; *what you think about* most of the time causes *how you feel* most of the time. If you think positive thoughts most of the time, you will feel good most of the time; if you think negative thoughts most of the time, you will feel bad most of the time. Thinking negative thoughts keeps you stuck in the anger process (in the river), because negative thoughts lead to bad feelings, and bad feelings are anger triggers.

In this chapter, you will learn some ways to deal with negative thoughts that keep you angry. You will learn how to think positive thoughts that make you feel self-empowered.

LESSON 1 ~ Maintain a Positive Mental Focus

What you focus on mentally is what you are thinking about at any given time. You look at certain mental images in your mind and you listen to certain mental sounds. That is what *thinking* means. In a sense, it is like watching old videos and listening to old tapes. You *think* in images and sounds. Most of the time you are not aware of what you are thinking about, but you must learn to be aware of what you think about. What kind of videos do you watch inside your mind most of the time? What kind of tapes do you listen to?

As a person with an anger problem, chances are you focus on negative thoughts most of the time. You look at mental images and videos that you associate with anger and violence. You may focus on mental images and watch mental videos that show how someone hurt you in the past. You may listen to mental tapes you associate with anger and rage, such as old mental tapes of what someone said that hurt you. Thinking about these images, videos, and tapes consistently means that you maintain a negative mental focus.

The mental images and videos you watch and the mental tapes you listen to act as *cues*. These mental images, videos, and tapes *cause the feelings* that *trigger* your anger.

You must change your mental focus; you must change what you think about most of the time. You must notice the negative mental images and videos you watch and the negative mental tapes you listen to, and then you must change them. You must replace the negative mental images, videos, and tapes with positive mental images, videos, and tapes that make you feel positive feelings. You must select mental images, videos, and tapes that will make you feel relaxed, or that will make you feel calm, confident, or assertive.

A Message from Bill

I didn't realize how much time I spent thinking negative thoughts. When I started paying attention, I found I consistently thought about things that made me angry. I thought about what people had said or done in the past that hurt me. I thought about what I would do, or like to do, to pay them back. I saw images of them in my mind—big, bright, clear images. Then I imagined images in my mind of scenes of revenge; sometimes they were full-color movies with stereophonic sound! I listened to old mental tapes, too. I could remember every word someone said, especially if the words had hurt me. Most of the time I wasn't consciously aware when I was focusing so negatively; the mental images, movies, and tapes played out just below the surface. Sometimes I was aware of my negative mental focus. At these times, I can remember purposely holding on to the images and sounds, especially the revenge scenes and tapes, because they made me feel powerful. I discovered I focused on negative images and tapes at least 50 percent of the time.

You *can* change what you think about most of the time, and changing what you think about most of the time will change how you feel most of the time. You will feel less angry and more relaxed and calm. You will feel more confident and assertive.

The skills you learn in this chapter will help you change how you think; that is, the skills will help you change your mental focus. The skills will help you stop focusing on mental images, videos, and tapes that cause the feelings that trigger your anger habit. The skills will help you maintain a positive mental focus. They will help you focus on mental images, videos, and tapes that will help you recover from your anger habit.

◆ **EXERCISE 1** What does it mean to change your mental focus?

_____

_____

_____

_____

_____

◆ **EXERCISE 2** The mental videos and tapes you *focus on* most of the time are what you *think about* most of the time. Chances are you often think negative thoughts. You focus on mental videos and mental tapes that make you feel anger triggers.

Identify a mental video you watch, or a mental tape you listen to much of the time, that makes you feel anger triggers. Describe that video or tape.

_____

_____

_____

_____

_____

_____

_____

_____

_____

LESSON 2 ~ The Skills

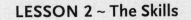 SKILL 1 | Look at Special Photos or Pictures

You have learned how focusing consistently on mental images that you associate with anger keeps you stuck in the anger habit. Now you will learn how to change your mental focus.

Do you have a special photo you carry in your wallet or purse that makes you feel good when you look at it? Maybe you have a photo of your significant other, or of one of your children. Maybe you have a picture from nature that makes you feel good, or a picture of a religious subject. If you don't have a special photo or picture that you carry, you should obtain one. Then when a trigger occurs, look at the photo or picture that makes you feel good, and as you look at it, relax your posture and slow down your breathing. You will automatically start feeling whatever good feelings you associate with the special photo or picture. If you associate a proud feeling with the person or thing in the special photo or picture, then you will automatically feel that feeling.

◆ **EXERCISE 1** Make a list of special photos or pictures you could use to deal with anger triggers. Then obtain such a photo or picture and keep the special photo or picture on your person.

_____

_____

_____

_____

_____

◆ **EXERCISE 2** Think of something in the past that made you angry. Thinking about it will make you feel some of the anger again. When you begin to feel some of that anger, follow the steps below:

    A. Look at your special photo or picture.

    B. Relax your posture.

    C. Slow down your breathing.

◆ **EXERCISE 3** On a scale from 1 to 10, what was your level of anger when you felt triggered? What is it after you use this new skill to change your mental focus?

_____

_____

_____

～ SKILL 2 | Listen to Relaxing Music ～

Listening to relaxing music changes how you feel. It has sometimes been said that music "soothes the wild beast." Some people compare their anger habit to a wild beast. Does it sometimes feel that way to you? You may find relaxing music to be a good way to quiet the wild beast inside of you. Listening to relaxing music will help you maintain a positive mental focus. Listening to aggressive music, for example, "gangster rap," will have the opposite effect—it will wake up the wild beast.

◆ **EXERCISE 1** What kind of music do you find relaxing? Slow ballads, classical, New-Age? Make a list.

_____

_____

_____

_____

_____

_____

◆ **EXERCISE 2** Find a CD or audiotape that you find relaxing, and play it. How does the CD or tape make you feel?

_____

_____

_____

_____

_____

_____

◆ **EXERCISE 3**

A. Sit next to a tape player or CD player. Put your relaxing tape or CD in the player. Don't start the tape or CD just yet.

B. Now think of something that made you angry in the past. Rate the level of your anger using a scale from 1 to 10.

C. When you begin to feel some anger, start the tape or CD and listen to the relaxing music. Listen to the music for five to ten minutes.

What is your anger level after listening to the tape or CD for five to ten minutes?

_____

∾ SKILL 3 | Use Humor to Interrupt Triggers ∾

Humor is a powerful way to interrupt anger triggers, a good way to get out of the river, and a good anchor. Even when you are close to the Falls, humor can get you out.

A man called Norman Cousins suffered from a disease that caused him a lot of pain. Cousins didn't want to use pain medication, because he believed it would have a negative effect on his recovery. But he felt powerless over the pain and that feeling of powerlessness made him angry. As a way to deal with the pain, Cousins borrowed old comedy movies from the library. He discovered that watching a humorous movie for two hours not only provided him with two hours of pain-free time, but also relieved his anger!

A Message from Jennifer

My name is Jennifer. I live in Knoxville, Tennessee. I've used anger like a drug for a long time. But I'm working a program now, and I'm doing a lot better. Soon after I began my recovery, I saw how my mental focus affected me. I've learned some skills to change my focus. First I learned to pay attention to what I was thinking; then I learned how to change my thoughts. I had maintained a negative mental focus most of my life, so it wasn't easy to change. It took practice. I had to continue to pay attention to what I thought about, and I had to keep applying the skills I learned to change my focus. I'm still practicing these skills. I suppose I'll have to practice them the rest of my life, but that's okay with me. I'm able to control my anger better than I ever thought I could.

◆ **EXERCISE 1** Watching a humorous video is a good way to deal with anger triggers. Borrow a humorous video from the library, or buy one at a discount store. Watch the video. How does watching a humorous video make you feel?

_____

_____

_____

_____

_____

◆ EXERCISE 2

A. Put your humorous video in a video player. Don't start the video just yet.

B. Now think of something that made you angry in the past. Measure the level of your anger on a scale from 1 to 10.

C. Now start the video. Watch at least ten minutes of the video.

After watching the video for ten minutes, what is your anger level? What is the level of your anger after twenty minutes? After sixty minutes? What is your level of anger after watching the entire video?

_____

_____

_____

_____

◆ Listen to a Humorous Audiotape

Listening to a humorous audiotape is also an effective anger management tool. Like watching a humorous video, it will help you maintain a positive mental focus.

◆ **EXERCISE 1** Borrow or buy a humorous audiotape, and listen to the tape. How does listening to the humorous tape make you feel?

_____

_____

_____

_____

_____

_____

Note: Avoid using videos and audiotapes that use verbal or physical violence.

◆ **EXERCISE 2**

A. Put your humorous audiotape in a tape deck. Don't start the tape just yet.

B. Now think of something that made you feel angry in the past. What is your level of anger on a scale from 1 to 10?

C. When you start feeling some of the anger, start the tape and listen to it for at least ten minutes.

After listening to the humorous audiotape for ten minutes, what is your anger level? What is it after twenty minutes? What is it after listening to the entire tape?

_____

_____

_____

_____

◆ **EXERCISE 3** Is humor a good anchor for you, a good way to get out of the anger process? What other ways can you use humor as an anchor?

_____

_____

_____

_____

_____

_____

_____

_____

_____

∾ SKILL 4 | Use Physical Exercise to Interrupt Anger Triggers ∾

Exercise is another good way to interrupt an anger trigger; it is another effective anchor. Of course, before starting an exercise program you should check with your doctor.

There are many types of exercises from which to choose. Choose one that is affordable and that you can do easily without a lot of equipment. Choose a form of exercise you feel you will be most likely to use. Exercise usually puts you in a good mood, and when you are in a good mood, you automatically think positive thoughts. Therefore, exercise is another good way to help you maintain a positive mental focus.

There are many forms of exercise that you could use to interrupt anger triggers. The following are some examples:

- Pump iron
- Walk
- Run
- Clean house
- Do push-ups
- Chop wood
- Do deep knee bends

Some of the types of exercise listed above may appeal to you, or none of them may appeal to you. You must think of types of exercise that you would like to do.

◆ **EXERCISE 1** List at least two types of physical exercise you would be willing to use.

_____

_____

◆ **EXERCISE 2** Use one of the physical exercises you listed the next time you feel an anger trigger. What effect does it have? Does it interrupt the trigger? Is it a good anchor?

_____

_____

_____

∾ SKILL 5 | Make a Gratitude List ∾

It is easy to forget the good things you have in your life, especially in times of stress. When you feel stressed, your mental focus often becomes negative.

Maintaining awareness of the good things in your life creates a positive mental focus; it makes you feel grateful. If you are aware of some of the good things in your life, you will be less likely to get angry when a trigger happens. But you need a way to be aware of the good things in your life. Making a gratitude list that you can look at will help you stay aware of the good things. You can look at your gratitude list and see what you have to be grateful for. It will allow you to make a useful comparison: You can compare the things on your gratitude list to whatever is triggering your anger, and that will help you keep things in perspective. It will help you see what is really important in your life and what is not.

A gratitude list will help you maintain a positive mental focus. The following is a list of things that anyone should be grateful for:

- being alive
- having eyes and ears
- having food to eat
- being able to breathe
- being able to talk

Chances are, you have all of the things in the above list in your life. If you had just one of the things listed, you would probably feel grateful for that one thing. But there must be many other things you have that you are grateful for, too.

◆ **EXERCISE** Make a list of things you are grateful for, and make three copies of the list. Keep one copy on your person, keep a copy on your nightstand, and tape a copy to the wall next to the bathroom mirror. Each time you feel triggered into the anger process, read your gratitude list.

I am grateful for...

_____

_____

_____

_____

_____

_____

_____

_____

_____

_____

A Message from Bill

Sometimes I made a gratitude list right on the spot. Sometimes I made the list just in my mind. I had a list that I wrote down and carried in my wallet on the back of a business card. But sometimes I couldn't get to my list—when I was driving my car, for example, or when I was in a room full of people and didn't want to look conspicuous. At those times, I made a mental list of the things I was grateful for. I'd just ask myself, "What am I grateful for, right now?" The list would begin to unfold in my mind. That skill got me out of the river every time I used it. It was a good anchor, and continues to be.

∽ SKILL 6 | Use Self-Commands to Interrupt Triggers ∽

You can use brief self-commands to interrupt your anger triggers. A self-command is a word or short phrase that helps you change negative feelings into positive feelings quickly. Self-commands make good anchors; use them to pull yourself out of the river.

The following are some examples of self-commands you can use to interrupt anger triggers:

- Change your breathing!
- Anger is pain!
- Violence is never justified!
- Stop!

When you use one of your self-commands, you must do it with feeling; you must put energy into it. You don't have to yell, but use a strong, assertive voice. You can say the command silently, if circumstances make it inappropriate to say it out loud. If you utter the self-command silently, you can still say it with feeling. Inside your mind, it should sound like a loud thought.

◆ **EXERCISE 1** Copy the self-commands listed. Write them on something small enough to fit into your wallet, on the back of a business card, for example.

◆ **EXERCISE 2**

A. Look at your list of self-commands. Choose a word or phrase from the list to use as a tool to interrupt your anger.

B. Now think of something that made you angry in the past. Measure the level of your anger on a scale from 1 to 10.

C. When you feel some of the anger, look at the self-command you chose.

D. Using a strong voice, say the self-command; say it with feeling.

◆ **EXERCISE 3** Using a scale from 1 to 10, rate the effect your self-command had on your anger.

_____

◆ **EXERCISE 4** Think of two or three other self-commands you could use, and write them down. Don't forget to add them to the list you will carry with you.

_____

_____

_____

You have learned some ways to maintain a positive mental focus. You have learned some skills to interrupt anger triggers. The new skills you have acquired represent choices. Refer to the list you made in Chapter 7, and add the new choices you have just learned to the list.

A Message from Tommy

My name is Tommy. I'm from Washington, D.C.

I knew I had an anger habit, and I knew I wanted to recover. I'd start the day in a positive frame of mind. I'd say to myself, "Today I'm not going to be stupid. I'm not going to go over the Falls." Then some little thing would happen, or maybe a lot of little things would happen in a row, and before I knew it, wham! Over the Falls. I needed skills. I needed a lot of anchors. I learned some of the skills in this chapter, and then things got better. Finally, I had things to do that would work. With my new skills, I could get out of the river before it was too late. Then I learned some more skills and added them to the ones I already knew. My box of anger management tools got bigger and I felt more able to manage my behavior. Later, things got even better. The more skills I learned, the better things got.

10

What to Avoid

It is important to know how to interrupt triggers and get out of the anger process. It is also important to know what to avoid.

In Chapter 9 you learned some specific hands-on skills to help yourself interrupt the anger process and get out of the river before it's too late. In this chapter you will learn that if you avoid certain things, people, places, and circumstances, you are less likely to end up angry in the first place.

LESSON 1 ~ Avoid Alcohol and Other Drugs

Alcohol or other drug use is involved in more than 50 percent of cases of family violence and in more than 50 percent of assaults and murders. Alcohol, cocaine, barbiturates, and some tranquilizers intensify the feelings that trigger anger. If you sincerely want to stop using anger, rage, and violence, you should abstain from alcohol and from all other drugs not prescribed by a physician. You must be careful even when using prescribed drugs.

If you now use prescribed medication, do not stop taking the medication without consulting a physician. Use your medication only as prescribed. Read the warnings on the labels. If the medication seems to make your anger worse, bring it to the attention of your physician.

Combinations of certain drugs are even more dangerous; for example, the use of alcohol combined with cocaine or barbiturates (sleeping pills). You cannot afford to use substances that will make your anger worse.

Alcohol definitely makes anger worse. Just a couple of drinks interfere with your judgement, making you more likely to say and do angry things. Use of other drugs, such as cocaine and speed, have the same effect; they impair thinking and make anger worse. When you use alcohol or other drugs, you are less likely to use your anger management skills.

Some people who have an anger problem use alcohol and other drugs in order to intensify their anger.

A case that illustrates the deadly effects of mixing alcohol with barbiturates occurred in 1966. A sailor got drunk in Chicago, Illinois, on a mixture of alcohol and sleeping pills. He went into a rage and murdered eight student nurses. He did not even remember the episode. He died in prison in the 1980s.

You are strongly urged to stop using all mood-altering drugs unless prescribed by a physician, including marijuana. If you associate marijuana with peaceful feelings, you are making a big mistake. Marijuana users who have a problem with anger are also violent. The risk is highest when your supply of the drug runs out, or when you are in situations where you cannot use the drug. At those times, your baseline tension level climbs above normal. Feelings of fear, anxiety, and frustration (anger triggers) intensify when the level of marijuana in your blood decreases. *If you have a problem with alcohol or other drugs, seek help now.*

◆ **EXERCISE 1** Why are you strongly urged to abstain from alcohol and other drugs?

_____

_____

_____

_____

◆ **EXERCISE 2** Do you drink or use other drugs? What drugs (including alcohol) do you use?

_____

_____

_____

_____

◆ **EXERCISE 3** Did you use alcohol or other drugs in the past but have now stopped? What drugs (including alcohol) did you use?

_____

_____

_____

_____

◆ **EXERCISE 4** Think about times when you used alcohol or other drugs when you were angry. Were you ever violent when drinking? Were you ever violent when using other drugs?

_____

_____

_____

_____

LESSON 2 ~ Avoid Places Where Heavy Drinking or Drug Use Takes Place

Most violence that ends in injury or death takes place where there is heavy drinking or drug use. Even if you don't use alcohol or other drugs, you are still at high risk for acting out angry feelings if you hang out where alcohol and other drugs are used. Those at the bar or party who are under the influence may say or do something to trigger you.

◆ **EXERCISE 1** Have you ever been violent in a place where there was heavy alcohol or drug use, even when you were not drinking or using other drugs? Explain.

_____

_____

_____

◆ **EXERCISE 2** For your entertainment you may depend on places where alcohol or other drugs are used. Where else could you go for entertainment?

_____

_____

_____

_____

_____

A Message from Craig

My name is Craig. I'm from Boston. I was addicted to alcohol and other drugs before I knew I had an anger habit, too. I rode with a biker gang. After I got clean and sober, I still hung out in the bar where the biker gang hung out. I was starting to take a look at my anger habit, but it was not a very close look. I have to admit that.

One night I was in the bar having a soft drink. All my friends were there. Someone said something to me—I can't even remember what it was. Whatever he said made me feel embarrassed. Embarrassment has always been one of my major anger triggers. The person who embarrassed me was drunk. I told him to apologize; he wouldn't. We argued, then fought. We both left before the cops came. The whole thing made me feel stupid, because when I thought about it, I knew I had set myself up just by being there at the bar. But I learned from the experience. I never went back to that or any other bar.

LESSON 3 ~ Avoid the Use of Anabolic Steroids (Growth Drugs)

Some professional athletes have been using steroids (growth drugs) since the 1960s. Steroids increase body strength and muscle mass, no doubt about it. Weight lifters and body builders were the first to use steroids, and the use of them has become widespread in recent years. Among teenagers, steroid use is increasing at an alarming rate.

There is no doubt that steroids improve athletic performance. But the use of steroids has some bad side effects. Steroids can cause serious health problems, such as strokes and heart attacks.

A Message from Terry

My name is Terry. I'm addicted to anger. I'm doing better now, a lot better. It's been a long time since I went to jail because of my anger.

My anger problem started before I was a teenager. At thirteen, I started lifting weights. I got strong real fast. Then a friend turned me on to steroids. The steroids made me even stronger, even faster. The steroids made me feel more confident, too. But I noticed they made my anger worse. After I got onto steroids, I started having trouble at school because of my anger. I got into a fight with a kid during gym class one day. I went completely out of control, in a fit of "'roid rage." I beat the kid up so bad, they had me arrested. I got expelled for a whole semester and got put on probation for two years. I felt ashamed and stupid. If you have a problem with anger, or if you're addicted to anger, don't use steroids. Man, just don't.

Steroid use has another serious side effect. Steroids are strongly linked to anger outbursts and increased aggression. People who use steroids are much more likely to be violent. This is true even for people who don't otherwise have a problem with anger. Steroid users call it "'roid rage." Steroid use by people who have an anger habit is especially dangerous.

◆ **EXERCISE** You have an anger habit. Why shouldn't you use steroids?

_____

_____

_____

_____

_____

LESSON 4 ~ Avoid Other People Who Have Problems with Anger and Rage

You are strongly urged to stop associating with other angry people, especially if they are not willing to change their behavior. Continuing to associate with people who are unwilling to do something about their anger will keep you stuck in your old anger pattern.

Some of your family members may have anger problems, your employer may have anger problems, or other people you cannot avoid may have anger problems. In these instances, you can only work your recovery program all the harder. But whenever possible, avoid people who are still stuck.

◆ **EXERCISE** Are some people you associate with stuck in anger and rage? What can you do, specifically, to stay away from them, or to spend less time with them if you cannot avoid them altogether.

_____

_____

_____

_____

LESSON 5 ~ Avoid Watching Violence in the Media

The mass media shapes behavior—this is obvious. The media presents role models who use violence to get what they want. The media presents images of violence over and over again. The media helps create the violence that threatens to tear society apart. It seems to make heroes out of killers. If nothing else, it gives violent people a lot of attention.

Watching violent movies and violent television shows will increase your anger. Playing violent video games will increase your aggression. Reading books or newspaper articles with violent themes will have the same result. Popular songs that glamorize violence will also make your problem worse.

You are strongly urged to reduce your exposure to media violence. Carefully select what you watch, what you read, and what you listen to.

Television news programs often show many images about negative events. The images associated with the negative events often produce feelings that are triggers for anger. For example, after watching the news, you may experience feelings of frustration or fear. The big, bright, full-color images presented on television make a much stronger impression on the brain than do written words in the newspaper. These stronger visual images are harder for the brain to forget, and they produce stronger, longer-lasting feelings. You may want to stop watching television news and listen to radio news or read the newspaper instead.

◆ **EXERCISE 1** Think of the last time you watched a violent TV program or movie. How did it make you feel? Did you notice an increase in baseline tension in your body?

_____

_____

_____

_____

◆ **EXERCISE 2** You may depend on television and movies for entertainment. What else could you do for entertainment?

_____

_____

_____

_____

LESSON 6 ~ Avoid Venting

Venting includes yelling, beating a pillow with your fists, or stomping your feet. Venting is physically aggressive action that is not directed at people, animals, or property. Venting was once thought to drain off the tension produced by anger. But you have an anger habit and the kind of venting described here is a part of your anger pattern. For you, venting is like practicing. Venting will only keep you stuck in the anger process; it will only keep you stuck in the river. People who do not use anger like a drug may safely vent once in a while, but as a person with a serious anger problem, you cannot safely vent. You must find other ways to deal with frustration and other anger triggers.

A Message from Sam

My name is Sam. I was born and raised in the Bronx. I did my anger right up front. I was loud and dramatic. I hit things. I threw things. When I first decided to stop the violence, I used venting as a way to deal with my anger. I pounded pillows. I broke useless things against the basement wall. I punched and kicked the heavy bag. Venting left me feeling drained and tired, but it didn't help me change my angry behavior. Venting made it worse. It reinforced my anger habit. I found other ways to deal with anger— I had to.

◆ **EXERCISE 1** Do you vent when angry? What do you do when you vent?

_____

_____

_____

_____

◆ **EXERCISE 2** Instead of venting, you could use the skills you are learning. Skills are choices, anchors. What skills could you use instead of venting? Make a list.

_____

_____

_____

_____

_____

_____

_____

LESSON 7 ~ Avoid Guns

More than 50 percent of murders are committed by angry people who own guns. If you own guns or other weapons, you are strongly urged to dispose of them appropriately. The reason you should dispose of your weapons is obvious.

◆ **EXERCISE 1** If you own weapons, what purpose do they serve? Do you really need them?

_____

_____

_____

_____

_____

_____

_____

◆ **EXERCISE 2** If you own weapons, are you willing to give them up? If you are not willing to give up your weapons, why aren't you?

_____

_____

_____

_____

_____

_____

◆ **EXERCISE 3** If you are willing to give up your weapons, how will you do it?

_____

_____

_____

_____

_____

11

Special Methods and Skills for Managing Anger

∾ Anger Cues ∾

In Chapter 10 you learned what to avoid in order to stay out of the anger process as much as possible. In this chapter, you will learn some special methods and skills to help you deal with persistent triggers. In this chapter you will also learn the difference between assertiveness and aggression.

What Are Cues?

Think back to Chapter 6, which explains the five stages of the anger process. The first stage is a cue—something you see or hear that signals you to do something. Cues exist all around us: An orchestra conductor "cues" each musician with a signal that tells them when to start or stop playing. A red light at a corner is a cue to stop. The sound of an ambulance siren is a cue to pull over to the curb. The smell of food cooking is a cue that tells your mouth to start producing saliva. Similarly, an *anger cue* signals your body and brain to produce an *anger trigger*. It tells your body and brain to produce a *bad feeling*. Some anger cues are memories of things you have seen or heard. They are called *memory cues*.

Memory Cues

Memories of things that happened to you also act as cues, and they can be as strong or stronger than cues that happen in the present. Remembering something you saw or heard "cues" you to feel the same feelings you had when it happened. Memories of bad things make you feel bad feelings again; memories of good things make you feel good feelings again.

Memories of things that produce negative feelings, like fear or frustration, act as anger triggers. Chances are you have many such memories—memories that cause you emotional pain when they pop into your mind, memories that act as cues. Memories that act as cues keep your tension level high and keep you stuck in the anger process. Some of the memories that are cues for the feelings that trigger anger are very stubborn. They pop into your conscious mind often, and it is hard to keep from focusing on them. But you can learn how to deal with memory cues that, in the past, kept you stuck in anger and rage; you can learn how to let go of them once and for all, so that they no longer produce the feelings that trigger your anger.

◆ Scenario 1

Think back to the Niagara Falls metaphor that's explained in Chapter 6. Suppose someone said something in the past that embarrassed you and that feeling of embarrassment triggered your anger, causing you to plunge into the Niagara River. Suppose some time has passed; you are walking down the street a few days later and happen to see that same person again. How do you suppose you would react? Do you think you would get angry all over again? Chances are you would. The person who embarrassed you would now become an anger cue. Seeing the person's face would cause you to feel embarrassed again. The person's face would act as a cue, causing you to recall what was said or done that produced the feeling of embarrassment. You would experience the feeling of embarrassment again, and that would trigger your anger all over again. The person's face would act as an anger cue until you did something to change the *cue*.

◆ Scenario 2

Suppose someone said something that caused you embarrassment, but you never saw the person again. Some time passes. You are walking down the street a few days later. You don't actually see the person on the street, but a memory of his face pops suddenly into your mind. Inside your mind, the memory looks big and bright. You even remember small details, perhaps the tiny scar on his cheekbone! Would the memory of the person who embarrassed you cause you to feel angry again? It would! Because acting as a cue, the memory would cause you to reexperience the feeling of embarrassment that triggered your anger at the time of the actual event. In other words, the memory would act as a cue. It would act as a *memory cue*, and the feeling of embarrassment would act as an *anger trigger*. You would get angry all over again.

LESSON 1 ~ Deal with Stubborn Memory Cues

You can learn how to deal with stubborn memory cues.

There are different kinds of memories, including visual memories and auditory memories. Visual memories are made up of certain qualities, such as brightness and size.

When you recall a visual memory, you see it like a picture or videotape projected on a screen inside your mind. The brightness of the image attached to a particular memory is a very important quality when it comes to recalling the memory. The brightness of the image that makes up a visual memory ranges from very bright to very dim.

All visual memories produce feelings. These feelings may be strong or weak, depending on how bright or dim the image of the memory looks to you when you see it on the screen inside your mind. Bright memories cause strong feelings; very bright memories cause very strong feelings. Dim memories cause weak feelings; very dim memories cause very weak feelings.

Most visual memories fade out and become dim and uninteresting with the passing of time, but not always. Sometimes memories remain very bright for a very long time, especially if they are the result of powerful events that made you feel very strong feelings in the first place. Old faded memories won't give you trouble. There is not enough brightness left to interest your brain. The faded-out memories slip down out of sight, down into the murky bottom layers of the mind, because their lack of brightness makes them too heavy to remain on the surface. These old, heavy, faded-out memories almost never pop back up to the surface.

Memory cues that remain very bright are the ones that will give you trouble, especially the ones you associate with strong negative feelings like fear. Their brightness makes them lighter; they float closer to the surface of your mind. Even bright memories won't give you trouble all of the time, but they are always lurking just below the surface. They knife through your conscious mind like sharks cutting the surface of the water, showing only their dorsal fin.

Trying to force down a big, bright memory won't work. It is like forcing a beach ball down under water. What happens when you let go? The beach ball pops back to the surface. Right? In fact, it often pops completely out of the water! That's what happens when you force down a big, bright memory. It pops back up as soon as you let go, and for a while it looks even bigger and brighter.

There is only one way to deal with a stubborn memory cue: Reduce the brightness of the image representing the memory. The skill below will help you reduce the brightness from any stubborn memory cue that keeps you stuck in the anger process. The skill changes the memory cue. It extinguishes it. It puts out the memory cue's light. Then the memory sinks below the surface, way down deep where it belongs, and it stays there. Practice the skill below with all of your stubborn memory cues. It is another way to change your mental focus.

◆ **EXERCISE 1** Make a list of your stubborn memory cues, the ones that create feelings that trigger your anger. An example of a stubborn memory cue might be one of the following:

■ A big, bright memory of someone who beat you up when you were a kid. When you think of the person, you feel strong feelings of fear and anxiety, and then you get angry.

■ A big, bright memory of someone who did something that caused you to feel rejected. When you think of that person you feel rejected again, and then you get angry.

■ A big, bright memory of something that happened that caused you to feel disappointed. You think of the memory, feel disappointed, and then get angry.

■ A big, bright memory of yourself doing something that resulted in a personal loss. You feel stupid and then you get angry.

Now make a list of your stubborn memory cues.

_____

_____

_____

_____

_____

◆ **EXERCISE 2** Select one of the memory cues you listed, and then follow the steps below. You may have to close your eyes to do some of the steps. If you need to close your eyes, you may open them long enough to read the next step. With practice, you will not need to look at the steps. You will be able to do the skill from memory.

Note: This is a difficult skill, but an important one. Ideally, you should have someone read the steps to you, perhaps a counselor or your Pathways to Peace mentor. Once you have mastered this skill, you will have a way to deal effectively with any memory cue that threatens to keep you stuck in anger and rage. Many of your strongest angry feelings are the result of memory cues attached to bad things that happened to you in the past. If you have suffered severe trauma in the past, you may not be able to completely heal from anger and rage until you resolve the trauma. This skill is designed to help you resolve trauma.

1. Pretend you have a movie screen inside your mind. Think of the memory cue you want to change. Project it as a picture on the screen, and notice the brightness of the picture.

2. How angry does the memory cue make you feel? Rate the anger on a scale of 1 to 10.

3. Using your imagination, very quickly increase the brightness of the picture until the screen goes blank and the picture disappears, the way the picture on a TV screen disappears when you twist the brightness knob all the way up.

4. Let the picture fade back in. Notice that the picture has lost some of its brightness. Also, notice your feeling of anger has lost some of its intensity. Rate your anger on the 10-point scale.

5. Now increase the brightness of the picture quickly, as before, until the screen goes blank again. Let the picture fade back in. Notice that the picture has lost more brightness and your feeling of anger is even less intense. Rate your anger on the 10-point scale.

6. Repeat step five three more times, until your anger rates a 3 or less on a 10-point scale.

LESSON 2 ~ Learn to Change Your Posture, Breathing, and Voice

Your posture, along with how you breathe and use your voice, creates whatever emotional state you happen to be in at a given moment in time. Every feeling you experience is connected to these three parts of your behavior. You cannot stay angry unless you use your body, breath, and voice in an angry way.

When you are angry, this is what you do:

- You maintain a rigid posture.

- You breathe rapidly in your upper chest.

- You speak rapidly in a loud, high-pitched voice.

This posture, breathing pattern, and way of using your voice reinforces anger. In fact, this pattern *creates* your anger. This pattern sends a specific message to the brain, telling it to make stimulating chemicals associated with angry behavior. The pattern tells the brain to stimulate the glands to produce large amounts of adrenaline. Normally you are not consciously aware of your posture, how you breathe, or how you use your voice, but you can learn how to be consciously aware. If you learn how to be consciously aware of these three parts of your behavior, you will have a powerful way to change how you feel. You will have a powerful way to change an anger trigger into a feeling that moves you toward recovery from anger and rage instead of back into violent behavior.

Changing your posture, breathing, and voice changes how you feel. Here are the three steps. When you feel angry, do the following three things:

A Message from Frank

I'm Frank, from Little Rock. I thought this skill was too simple to work. I thought everything had to be difficult and complicated—talk about limiting beliefs! But I tried it and found out that changing my posture, breathing, and voice is the easiest and fastest way to change a negative feeling (trigger) and to get out of the river. It's an easy skill to learn, but you have to be consistent. After a while, it becomes automatic.

At first, I took it one piece at a time. I started by paying attention to my breathing. When I felt a trigger, I told myself to slow down my breathing and to breathe from my belly not up in my chest (that's how I breathe when I'm angry). After I got good at changing my breathing, then I started paying attention to my posture, too; then I started paying attention to how I was using my voice. I found that just changing my breathing was often enough. When I changed my breathing, my posture and voice changed, too. I don't even have to think about it now.

---

1. First, relax your body. Lean to one side or sit down.

2. Next, slow down your breathing, and breathe more deeply, down in your belly.

3. Then, slow down your rate of speech, and reduce the volume and pitch of your voice; speak more softly and use a deeper tone.

Changing your posture, breathing, and voice in the way described above will change how you feel. It will make you feel more relaxed and calm. It sends a different message to the brain. It tells the brain to stop making chemicals associated with angry behavior and tells it to make chemicals associated with relaxation instead. Making these changes in your posture, breathing pattern, and voice interrupts the anger process.

◆ **EXERCISE 1** Describe how you use your posture, your breathing, and your voice when you are angry.

_____

_____

_____

_____

_____

_____

◆ **EXERCISE 2** There are three steps to changing how you feel by changing your posture, breathing, and voice. Describe the three steps to change your angry feelings.

1. _____

_____

2. _____

_____

3. _____

_____

LESSON 3 ~ Recite a Brief Poem or Prayer

This skill works best if you breathe slowly and deeply as you recite the poem or prayer.

◆ **EXERCISE** Write down a favorite brief poem or prayer you could use to deal with triggers. Practice using this skill each time you feel an anger trigger.

_____

_____

_____

_____

_____

_____

_____

LESSON 4 ~ Read a Joke Book or Scan a Book of Cartoons

Did anyone ever say or do something humorous that reduced your anger? If so, then you know the power of humor to deal with anger triggers. Keep joke books and cartoon books handy. Use them as tools to deal with anger triggers.

A Message from Ellie

My name is Ellie. I'm from the Midwest. I had a bad problem with anger. I've been in recovery now for over a year, and I'm doing a lot better. Early in my recovery, I found out how much humor could help. I had a friend who wasn't addicted to anger. Her name was Jill. She knew I was addicted to anger and was trying to recover. My friend knew a million jokes and was good at telling them. I thought I could make good use of Jill's skills. I figured I could call her when I was triggered, then ask her to tell me a joke. I thought the humor would act as an anchor to yank me out of the river. I told Jill about my scheme, and she agreed to help. From then on, whenever I felt triggered and I was near a phone, I'd call Jill and yell, "Tell me a joke. Quick!" It worked even better than I thought it would, even when I was in white water right down near the brink of the Falls. The trick was remembering to make the call.

◆ **EXERCISE 1** Do you know a person who you could call who would tell you a joke a or funny story when you need it, like the friend Ellie called (see page 138)?

_____

What kind of joke book or cartoon book would be helpful to you?

_____

_____

_____

◆ **EXERCISE 2** You can also use humorous things that actually happened. Can you remember a humorous thing that makes you laugh every time you think of it? If you can, write it down. Then you can read it to yourself when you are triggered.

_____

_____

_____

_____

_____

_____

_____

_____

_____

_____

_____

LESSON 5 ~ Aggression vs. Assertiveness

Being Aggressive

When you are aggressive, you are hostile. It means you are saying or doing something that is harmful. Angry words are aggressive words; angry behavior is aggressive behavior.

You must replace aggressive statements and behaviors with assertive statements and behaviors.

Examples of Aggressive Statements

"You're stupid!"

"You don't know what you're talking about!"

"You better stop that right now!"

"If you say that again, you'll be sorry!"

Examples of Aggressive Behaviors

- adopting threatening posture
- jabbing at someone's chest with your finger
- throwing something
- hitting or kicking something or someone
- shoving or pushing someone
- breaking something

◆ **EXERCISE 1** Write down three examples of aggressive statements that you have used.

_____

_____

_____

◆ **EXERCISE 2** Write down three examples of aggressive behaviors that you have used.

_____

_____

_____

Being Assertive

When you are *assertive,* it means you are making a statement; it means you are declaring something. It means you are saying something or doing something that makes a statement about how you feel. Assertive statements and behaviors are nonthreatening; they do not scare people or put people on the defensive.

◆ Assertive Statements

An assertive statement will let the listener know what you need or how you feel, and it will usually not cause the person to react in a negative way.

Examples of Assertive Statements:

"When you said I was stupid, I felt hurt."

"When you said I was too skinny, I felt rejected."

"When you said I wasn't going to get that raise in pay, I felt disappointed. Then I felt angry."

"When you made fun of me in front of my friends, I felt embarrassed."

"When you lied to me, I felt disrespected."

Other Examples of Assertive Statements:

"I don't want to do that."

"I don't want you to talk to me in that tone of voice."

"Please stop making fun of me; I don't like it."

◆ How to Use Your Voice When Making an Assertive Statement

Assertive statements require using your voice in a certain way. An assertive voice is a nonthreatening voice but not a wimpy voice. Keep the following four guidelines in mind:

1. Use a strong voice, but not a loud voice.

2. Speak clearly.

3. Speak at a normal rate, not too fast.

4. Use a lower voice tone, not high-pitched.

◆ Assertive Behaviors

Assertive behaviors require using your body in a certain way. You must use an *assertive posture* and *assertive gestures.* An assertive posture and assertive gestures are nonthreatening, but they are not submissive.

Examples of Assertive Behaviors:

- answering a question using a calm, clear voice

- raising your voice slightly to emphasize disappointment

- making eye contact and leaning forward slightly when telling someone you feel frustrated

Keep the following four guidelines in mind when you are using assertive behaviors:

1. Maintain an alert, but not tense, posture.

2. Make slower gestures, not quick and abrupt.

3. Make relaxed eye contact, don't stare intently.

4. Maintain a neutral expression, don't smile or scowl.

◆ **EXERCISE 1** Write down three examples of assertive statements. Make them different from the examples listed on page 141.

_____

_____

_____

A Message from Howard

My name is Howard. I've got a problem with anger, and it has cost me a lot. I hurt a lot of people with my angry words and angry behavior. I feel bad about it. But I'm doing better now.

I didn't know the difference between aggression and assertiveness. I thought anything short of hitting someone or throwing something was being assertive. I didn't count verbal threats as aggression; I didn't count threatening postures. Most of the time I didn't even know when I was using threatening words or postures. I had to learn to be aware of my words and my posture. I had to learn to be aware of the way I said things, too. I practiced listening to my own voice. I tuned into how loud I spoke and to the tone of my voice. I learned to pay attention to my posture. I found out I sounded and looked pretty aggressive even when I wasn't trying to be. When I was just trying to be assertive, I spoke too loud. My voice tone was too high. I spoke too fast. Then I began to change how I spoke so that I would not sound so aggressive. I noticed I often stood too close to people I was talking to. I often leaned too far forward. Then I changed how I used my posture, and that made me look less aggressive. I also noticed how I used my eyes. I saw I often made too much eye contact. I drilled other people's eyes with mine when I talked to them. So I stopped doing that so much. I learned how to break eye contact once in a while.

◆ **EXERCISE 2** Write down three examples of assertive behaviors different from those listed on the previous page.

_____

_____

_____

LESSON 6 ~ Take a Respite

You are learning new ways to respond to triggers. But sometimes you will feel like you are on "trigger overload." Things can pile up and seem overwhelming. At such times you may need to *take a respite*. To take a respite means to take time out. Usually it means taking an overnight break from a stressful situation, for example, a situation that causes you to feel frustrated or anxious, so that your angry feelings won't be triggered.

Taking a respite does not mean you are running away. It is taking time out—time out to think things through, time out to calm down. Sometimes you may need to get out of the situation entirely for a brief time.

Sometimes a short respite is enough. You could go away for an hour or two. You could take a walk or go to a movie. You could go for coffee with your Pathways to Peace mentor (you will learn about Pathways to Peace mentors later in this guidebook). Sometimes you may need to get away for a day or two. Think this over carefully. Talk about it with a friend or with your Pathways to Peace mentor before you make a decision to take a lengthy respite.

A respite is not defeat. Taking a respite is one of your choices; it is another anchor to throw on shore, another way to get out of the river. You could add "take a respite" to your list of choices.

Before you take a brief respite or a longer one, tell someone what you are doing and why. Tell them when you plan to return. Remember, you still have to be accountable.

◆ **EXERCISE 1** What does it mean to *take a respite?*

_____

_____

_____

_____

_____

◆ **EXERCISE 2** Would taking a respite be a good choice for you? Why?

_____

_____

_____

_____

_____

◆ **EXERCISE 3** If you need to take a respite, where would you go? If you need to take a mini-respite, where would you go?

_____

_____

_____

_____

_____

◆ **EXERCISE 4** Who would you talk to for help in deciding whether or not to take a respite?

_____

_____

_____

_____

_____

LESSON 7 ~ Go to a Pathways to Peace Meeting

You will learn more about the Pathways to Peace program in the last chapter of this workbook. It is strongly suggested that you use this self-help program, because it will help assure your success in recovering from your anger habit.

Successful Pathways to Peace members attend meetings regularly. The meetings help you learn to deal with triggers. They help you learn the Pathways to Peace Principles. Of course, you will want to read the Pathways to Peace written materials, but you will need to attend Pathways to Peace meetings in order to reinforce what you learn from the text. Pathways to Peace members offer each other support, understanding, and friendship. Pathways to Peace program members know what you are going through.

◆ **EXERCISE** Is there a Pathways to Peace program in your area? If you don't already know the answer to this question, take a few minutes to look in the yellow pages under anger management programs, or consult the Pathways to Peace national office (contact information is listed on page 209 of this workbook). Where is it and when does it meet? How do you feel about going to your first Pathways to Peace meeting?

_____

_____

_____

_____

LESSON 8 ~ Establish and Use an Empowerment Cue or an Aversion Cue

You know that you have an anger habit. You know that you learned your anger habit by repeating angry behavior over and over. This kind of learning process is sometimes called *conditioning*. It is an example of *stimulus/response conditioning*.

The cue for your anger habit is a negative feeling, such as fear or frustration. The negative feeling is what fires off the anger process and plunges you into the river. It is the *stimulus*. The *response* to the trigger is your angry behavior.

There is another part to the conditioning process: the reward. You will not form a habit unless you are rewarded for the behavior. A reward is a feeling of pleasure. The reward for your angry behavior is the feeling of power you experience when you get angry and the pleasure that the power brings you. Power and pleasure are your rewards.

Each time you use anger and are rewarded by feeling powerful, your habit grows stronger. It is *reinforced*. When a habit is reinforced often enough, it becomes so strong that even when you use anger to feel powerful and it does not work, you will still want to repeat the same behavior. If you were not rewarded often when you first started using anger to feel powerful, you would not have developed a problem with anger. If you felt more pain than pleasure, your angry behavior would not have become a habit. Now you are learning that your angry behavior results in pain more often than it results in pleasure. That is one of the reasons you have a desire to change your behavior.

Now you want to change. You want to recover from your anger habit and stop behaving violently; you want to stop hurting people and damaging things. But now you find yourself still saying and doing angry things even though you have sincerely promised to stop angry behavior. That is the nature of a habit. You know you are addicted to something when you find yourself doing it even when you have decided not to do it.

The tools you will learn in this part of the workbook take advantage of the same conditioning process that your brain used to create your anger habit. You will learn some tools that will help you develop a new habit: *recovery* from your anger habit.

You learned about cues earlier, in Chapter 11. You learned about cues (signals) that cause triggers (negative feelings) that fire off your anger (see page 132). Now you will learn about another class of cues. You will learn about cues that lead to feelings that can *empower* you, instead of leading to limiting feelings that trigger anger. They are called *empowerment cues*.

An *empowerment cue* is a tool that helps people interrupt a limiting emotional state like anger. There are three varieties of empowerment cues: *visual, auditory,* or *kinesthetic*.

Visual Cue

A visual cue is something you can see. A picture of Jesus or Mohammed is an example of a visual empowerment cue. For some people, looking at a photo of Jesus or Mohammed causes them to have strong feelings of confidence and personal power.

Auditory Cue

An auditory cue is something you can hear. The sound of a rousing symphony like Beethoven's *Ninth* is an example of an auditory empowerment cue. Listening to the *Ninth*, especially the choral section at the end, makes some people feel empowered.

Kinesthetic Cue

A kinesthetic cue is something you can feel. Any object you can hold that gives you a positive feeling when you touch it is a kinesthetic empowerment cue. For example, some people carry a religious object in their pocket or around their neck, such as a cross or crucifix. They experience positive feelings when they touch the cross or crucifix.

◆ Establish an Empowerment Cue on Your Wrist

One of the disadvantages of using an object such as a cross or crucifix as an empowerment cue is that you may lose the object. Using the technique described below, you can learn how to connect an empowerment cue to a specific location on your body, such as your wrist. The advantage of this kind of empowerment cue is that you cannot lose the cue. This type of empowerment cue should be located on an appropriate area of the body. It is customary to place the cue on the wrist. Once established, the cue can be touched off as needed.

This empowerment cue technique is not as strange as it may sound at first. Most people find this technique fascinating as well as useful. They are often amazed at how well it works, and they grow to appreciate the feeling of self-empowerment the technique gives them.

To establish an empowerment cue on your wrist, use the following instructions:

1. Decide on which wrist you want to establish the cue. The right wrist is often best for a right-handed person.

2. Next, recall a memory of a time you felt empowered, for example, when you felt relaxed, confident, or proud. In your imagination, see, hear, and feel everything that went on.

   At the peak, when the empowered feeling is the most intense, grasp your wrist using your thumb and index finger; squeeze your wrist firmly for fifteen to twenty seconds, and then let go.

3. Now recall the event again. As soon as the feelings peak again, reconnect the cue with the same amount of pressure as before, at the exact same spot. Hold for fifteen to twenty seconds, and then let go. Establishing the cue again reinforces the original cue. The process should be repeated as often as needed in order to establish a strong empowerment cue. The cue must be strong (on a scale from 1 to 10, it should be at least an 8). Otherwise, the stimulus will end up being too weak; the nervous system will fail to link up the internal image with the response. You must make sure to reset the cue point at the same spot, applying the same amount of pressure with the finger and thumb, each time. If the same location is not used or if the pressure is varied, the brain will get

---

A Message from Bill

I helped someone connect a cue on his wrist as part of a demonstration in a group. He had a serious problem with anger and rage. In fact, he'd done prison time because of what he did to people while angry. He had no problem thinking of an image of a memory he associated with intense anger! He focused on the memory. His breath was rapid and ragged, high up in the chest, and his posture was rigid. The muscles in his face and neck quivered and pulsated. His face got bright red. The rest of the group grew uneasy watching him. I helped him establish a strong empowerment cue on his wrist connected to the memory; then I told him to fire the stimulus. Within sixty seconds he returned to normal, and the anger subsided. It was like watching Mr. Hyde transform himself back into gentle Dr. Jekyll.

different messages, and the link between the cue and the memory may not take place. At best, it will end up diluted and weak.

4. This is the testing step. In order to make sure the cue is strong enough, you must test the cue.

In order to test the cue, recall a time when you felt angry. When the angry feelings peak, fire the empowerment cue by squeezing the cue point on the wrist, using exactly the same pressure as was used to establish the link in the first place. The cue point should be held for at least thirty seconds. You may have to wait a little longer before letting go, depending on the strength of the cue and on the strength of the competing anger trigger. Generally, thirty to sixty seconds is adequate. At the end of thirty to sixty seconds, you should begin to notice a change, for example, your breathing should slow down. You may also notice a decreased heart rate. You will begin to feel less angry.

◆ Establish an Aversion Cue on Your Finger

In order to make major behavior changes, it is useful to have both the carrot and the stick. That means it's useful to have both a positive cue and a negative one. An *empowerment cue* is the *carrot;* it's a positive cue. An *aversion cue* is the same idea, except that it leads to a painful emotional response instead of a pleasurable response. An *aversion cue* is the stick.

The process used to establish an aversion cue is essentially the same as the one you just used to establish an empowerment cue. It is best to establish the aversion cue on the hand opposite the one on which the empowerment cue is located. If you established your empowerment cue on your right wrist, as suggested, then establish the aversion cue on your left hand, specifically on the large knuckle of the index finger of your left hand. This makes it easier for you to separate the two cues in your mind, so that there is no confusion regarding the use of the two cues.

To establish this aversion cue, use the following instructions:

1. Think of a time in the past when you experienced an anger trigger and anticipated experiencing a feeling of power as a result of using anger, but felt a great deal of emotional and/or physical pain instead. Instead of feeling powerful, you lost something of value. Maybe you went to jail and lost your freedom, or maybe you lost some teeth in a physical fight. You should choose an experience that was so bad, you ended up saying to yourself, "I just have to find a different way to react!"

2. At the peak, when you are reexperiencing the painful feelings of the original event, firmly squeeze the large knuckle on your left index finger using the thumb and index finger of your right hand. Maintain firm pressure for approximately thirty seconds, and then let go.

3. Now test the aversion cue. Think of something that would generate a craving to use anger. At the peak of the craving, squeeze the aversion cue, using the same pressure at the exact same location on the large knuckle of the index fin-

ger on the left hand. If the craving to use anger gets interrupted, you have succeeded in establishing the aversion cue.

4. If the craving is still active, reestablish a stronger aversion cue and retest. Continue using the skill until you have established a stimulus that will extinguish any persistent anger cue.

Once established, the aversion cue can be used any time you feel a strong desire to use anger or violence. When you fire the cue (always using the same pressure, at the same point on your index finger), you will tend to reexperience the same painful feelings.

Using your aversion cue will cause you to stop and think, "Do I want to use verbal or physical violence in this situation and end up with that consequence again? Do I want to put myself through that pain again?"

◆ **EXERCISE 1** Think of a time in the past when you used anger, expecting a lot of pleasure, and you ended up losing something so important you said, "I wish I knew another way to act!"

_____

_____

_____

_____

_____

_____

_____

_____

_____

_____

_____

_____

 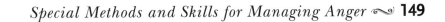

◆ **EXERCISE 2** Now that you have established a strong aversion cue, make a list of six to ten major anger cues. Take each cue, one at a time, and extinguish them using your aversion cue.

_____

_____

_____

_____

_____

_____

_____

_____

_____

_____

_____

_____

_____

_____

PART FOUR

Change Your Mind

12

Values

∾ Introduction ∾

This chapter begins the last part of the workbook. It represents a whole new phase of healing from your anger habit. Until now, most of the focus has been on helping you change your behavior. Changing your behavior is the work of your conscious mind. You had to use your conscious mind in order to acquire the skills you learned. In Chapter 7 you learned a three-step method for interrupting the anger process. In Chapter 8 you learned a relaxation method to help you deal more effectively with triggers. In Chapter 9 you learned how to change your mental focus as a way to stay out of the anger process. In Chapter 10 you learned what people, places, things, and situations you need to avoid in order to maintain an anger-free lifestyle. In Chapter 11 you learned some special methods and skills to help you deal effectively with anger cues.

This chapter, and the ones to follow, focus on helping you heal at a deeper level. You will learn how to make changes in your subconscious mind to make your healing more complete.

You have already learned about the power of your subconscious mind. For example, you now know that your anger habit, as well as all your other habits, is stored in your subconscious mind. In fact, your subconscious mind is a vast storehouse that holds information about everything you have ever seen, heard, tasted, smelled, or felt. Your subconscious mind holds all of your memories.

But your subconscious mind stores other things in its vast depths. It holds all of the higher parts of your whole self. It holds all of your *values* and *goals*, your *beliefs*, your sense of *mission*, and your feelings of *spirituality*. These are the parts of your whole self that really run the show. These parts represent your *higher self*, and they are what really determine your behavior. So in Chapters 12 through 16, you will be learning how to change these parts of your subconscious mind. Changing these parts will make it easier to change your angry behavior, and it will make it easier to keep your behavior changed.

Changing at the subconscious level of the whole self will take you to a higher level as a human being. You will be *transformed*.

LESSON 1 ~ Values and Recovery from Your Anger Habit

You learned a bit about values in Chapter 3 "The Eight Parts of the Whole Self." Now it is time to look closely at your values, because values influence your behavior. Actually, there are two kinds of values: *valued things* and *valued feelings*. You value certain things and you value certain feelings.

Valued Things vs. Valued Feelings

Of course you value things. You value your home and car, you value money. Who doesn't? You also value the people in your life. You value your friends, spouse, and children. The things and people you value and treasure are vehicles that move you toward your valued feelings and away from painful feelings. Valued feelings are positive feelings, like love or confidence; painful feelings are negative feelings, like fear or depression. As explained in Chapter 7, painful feelings (negative feelings) are anger triggers.

Valued Feelings

Freedom, security, and love are examples of *valued feelings*. This class of values is important to everybody. Psychologist William Glasser, author of *Reality Therapy*, lists three feelings all human beings must experience. He calls them the *"three A's of happiness."* They are *achievement, acceptance,* and *affection.* When you are unhappy, it is because your valued feelings are not being satisfied.

When you are angry, it is because you believe one of your valued feelings has been threatened or attacked.

A Message from Donna

My name is Donna. I'm an anger addict from Cincinnati. When I was full of anger and rage, I had no idea what my values were. I found out later my most valued feeling was anger. But I treated it as though it were a positive value. I used anger and rage to get high on my own brain chemicals; I used anger to feel powerful. I used anger to feel accepted by my peers, and I used it to fight off fear and anxiety. I wasn't aware of how short-lived the high was—it came and went in just a few seconds. But finally I became aware of how long the pain of the consequences lasted, and I became aware of how long the pain lasted for those I hurt. Like most anger addicts, I hurt my family most. That awareness of the pain that my behavior caused myself and others helped me see the importance of learning about values. I found out I had some *true* values, some *positive* values. I found out I had some values I could use that didn't result in pain for others or for myself.

Assume that freedom and power are two of your most valued feelings, and that having a car to drive gives you strong feelings of freedom and power. Suppose someone attacks your car by beating it with a sledgehammer and slashing the tires with a knife. Suppose the attack on your car makes you violently angry. Your anger would not be the result of the attack on your car. It would be the result of an attack on the *valued feelings* your car represents, namely, your feelings of *freedom* and *power*. Your brain would interpret the attack on your car as an attack on your personal freedom and personal power.

The following story about a real event illustrates the point. A man committed an assault. He was arrested and taken to jail. He felt a little fearful and ashamed as he was being led to the cell. He entered the cell, and then he heard the sound of steel meeting steel when the jailer slammed the cell door shut. That's when he suddenly realized what had just happened: He realized he had just lost his freedom! He said it wasn't until that moment that he understood just how much he valued his freedom. Immediately, he went into a rage.

Values influence how you act, they influence how you spend your time and energy, and they influence what goals you set. You were not born with a set of values; instead you arrived at your values through a learning process. You learned some of your values from teachers and peers, and others from movies and books. But you learned most of your values from your parents, or from whomever your caregivers were during the first ten or twelve years of your life.

Your anger habit has caused you to use anger like a *valued thing*, the way drug addicts use drugs as valued things. You have used anger like a drug to get high. You have used anger as a vehicle to satisfy one of your most valued feelings, the feeling of *power*.

Now you understand that anger is not a good vehicle to move you toward a feeling of power. Now you know that using anger like a drug causes more pain than pleasure; it causes pain for others and for yourself. Now you know you must find and use other vehicles to take you to your valued feelings. You must find other ways to feel powerful; you must find other ways to feel confident.

Identify Your Positive Values

This exercise will help you become aware of and identify your valued feelings. It will help you see how being aware of your values will have a positive effect on your commitment to heal from your anger habit.

For this exercise, you will need fifteen to twenty small pieces of paper. Make them about one inch high by about 1½ inches long. Don't worry about making the pieces of paper exactly one inch by 1½ inch—that's not important. Use a pencil so you can erase. You will need a flat surface on which to work. Follow the instructions closely.

◆ Examples of Valued Feelings

Here is a list of some examples of valued feelings that you can use to get started on the exercises below.

1. Contribution	7. Affection	13. Confidence
2. Freedom	8. Acceptance	14. Feeling connected
3. Feeling Loved/loving	9. Independence	15. Health
4. Serenity	10. Growth/growing	16. Peace
5. Accomplishment	11. Safety	17. Achievement
6. Security	12. Calm	18. Feeling liked

◆ EXERCISE 1

1. Ask yourself, "How do I want to feel every day as I live my new anger-free lifestyle?" Your first answer might be, "*Loved.* I want to feel loved every day of my life." Whatever your first answer is to the question, write it down on one of the pieces of paper. Write down whatever valued feeling comes to mind.

2. Then ask yourself, "What other feeling is important to me?" Your next answer might be, "I'd like to feel *excited* every day in whatever I do." Whatever your second answer may be, write it down on another piece of paper. In the beginning, don't bother trying to put your values in any kind of order; do that later. Just write them all down.

3. Now ask yourself, "What other feeling is important to me?" Your third answer might be, "Peaceful. I want to feel peaceful, at least some of the time, every day." Whatever your third answer is, write it down on another piece of paper.

4. Continue asking yourself the question, "What other feelings are important in my life?" until you have at least ten different feelings written down on ten different pieces of paper. Place them all on the pile with the others. Spend at least ten minutes on this part of the process.

5. Keep going until you cannot think of any more values, and then arrange your values according to what is most important to you. Here's how to arrange your values:

    A. Pick up the pieces of paper that you wrote your values on. Take the first two pieces and place them face up on the table or floor.

    B. Let's say the values written on the pieces of paper are love and freedom, respectively. Ask yourself, "What is more important in my life, love or freedom?" If the answer is love, place the piece of paper with the word "love" at the top to show it is in first position. Right underneath it, place the one with the word "freedom."

    C. Take the next piece of paper from the pile. Let's say the third one says "respect." Ask yourself again, "What is more important in my life, love, freedom, or respect?" If the answer is, "Respect is more important to me than freedom, but love is still more important than respect," then you will know you need to place respect second between love and freedom.

D. Continue arranging and rearranging your values according to what you feel is more important. Use all the pieces of paper you wrote your values on.

E. Now look at the arrangement. Ask yourself, "Are there any changes I want to make?" Keep rearranging your values until you know they are in the proper order. You will know by how the arrangement looks, sounds, and feels. If you feel no need to change the arrangement, consider this part of the exercise to be complete.

Find Your Breaking Point

There is one other important thing to recognize about values. There is a *breaking point* somewhere within their order of importance. For you, it could be at number six or seven. Maybe it would be number eight or nine. Whatever that place is for you, it is the point at which you would say, "Stop! You can't take that away from me! I can't live without that value!"

◆ **EXERCISE 2** Here is how to find your breaking point. Start with the last value on your arrangement. Ask yourself, "If I had all of the other good feelings, could I get along okay without this one?" If the answer is yes, go to the next one up the ladder of importance and ask the same question. Keep asking, "If I had all the other good feelings, could I get along okay without this one?" When you hear yourself say, "No! Absolutely not!"—*that* is your breaking point.

Now you know exactly what your values are and which ones are most important to you. You can use this knowledge to help yourself focus more effectively on what you really want out of life and what you want to avoid. You can use this knowledge to help yourself see more clearly why you want to stop using anger and rage once and for all.

Your *breaking point* has one other important meaning. Your breaking point, and all the values listed above it, is the value you will most likely get angry about if you think someone or something is threatening it. Whatever these values are, they will be threatened once in a while. That's life.

You must learn how to respond differently when any of your values are threatened.

◆ **EXERCISE 3** Now copy your list of values onto the form on the next page so you will have a permanent record. List your values in their proper order. Identify your cutoff value—your breaking point—by placing a star (*) next to it.

My Valued Feelings

1. _____
2. _____
3. _____
4. _____
5. _____
6. _____
7. _____
8. _____
9. _____
10. _____
11. _____
12. _____
13. _____
14. _____
15. _____
16. _____
17. _____
18. _____
19. _____
20. _____

13

Beliefs

Excessive anger isn't just a behavior problem. Verbally and physically abusive behavior is but a symptom, and the real problem goes deeper, much deeper. Your anger habit is also a belief problem. You could even say that your beliefs *run* your anger habit.

What Are Beliefs?

Beliefs are ideas that you have learned about yourself and your world. You have accepted your beliefs as true or false, right or wrong, or good or bad. But your beliefs are not necessarily facts. Beliefs are not things; they are more like strong feelings. Most of the time you are not aware of your beliefs, because they are stored in your subconscious mind.

Another way to think about beliefs is that they are the ideas that guide your life. Your beliefs give your life direction and meaning. They are convictions; therefore, beliefs are related to *faith.* You have *faith* in something when you *believe* in it. A belief is a *feeling* you have about whether something is true or false, good or bad, or right or wrong.

There are two kinds of beliefs: *positive beliefs* and *negative beliefs.*

◆ Positive Beliefs

Positive beliefs empower you. They open doors of possibility and they support you. They make you feel you are worthwhile; they make you feel others are worthwhile. They make you feel the world is worthwhile.

Positive beliefs tend to brighten your outlook. They give you confidence by helping you see the future in an optimistic light.

Positive beliefs make you feel good about yourself, others, and the world. Positive beliefs cause positive feelings, and *positive feelings keep you out of the river of anger and rage.*

◆ Negative Beliefs

Negative beliefs are toxic. Negative beliefs limit you, disempower you, and slam shut doors of possibility. They work against you by making you feel your life is not worthwhile. They make you feel others are not worthwhile, and they make you feel the world is not worthwhile. Negative beliefs cause you to make decisions and act in ways that harm others and yourself.

Negative beliefs tend to darken your outlook. They increase your fear and take away your confidence by causing you to see the future in a pessimistic light. Negative beliefs make you feel bad about yourself, other people, and the world. Negative beliefs cause negative feelings, and *negative feelings are triggers for your anger habit.*

How Did You Acquire Your Beliefs about Anger?

You were not born with your beliefs about anger—you learned them. You learned your beliefs from your parents, teachers, and peers. You learned them from the mass media (television, radio, newspapers, books). You learned some of your beliefs as a result of things that happened to you. Since beliefs are learned, you can give up old beliefs and learn new ones. But sometimes it is hard to let go of old beliefs, even when they no longer work for you.

Why You Must Change Your Beliefs

Think back to the Niagara Falls metaphor in Chapter 6. The metaphor shows why it is important to stay out of the river and away from the Falls. You have learned some skills to change your behavior; you have learned how to get out of the river. You learned how to change your breathing to stop the anger process quickly. You learned other skills so you wouldn't go over the Falls again. Those skills help you avoid negative results. But you need to make major belief changes, too. What if you continue to believe that anger is a good way to change how you feel? What if you continue to believe that anger means power? Those are the kinds of beliefs that have kept you stuck in your anger habit. Those are the beliefs that keep you in the river. To fully heal from addictive anger you must change your character. Since your beliefs are a major part of your character, you must remove the negative beliefs that keep you stuck and replace them with beliefs that support your recovery.

> **A man was asked to take part in an experiment about the power of belief.** The experiment used hypnosis. The man was hypnotized and went into a deep trance. A trance is like being very relaxed but still awake. While the man was in the trance, he was told he would be touched on the arm with a piece of hot metal but he was actually touched with a piece of ice. A blister formed at the point on his arm where he believed he was touched with hot metal.

Beliefs have a powerful influence in your life. The power of your beliefs affects all other recovery levels, even the biological level.

Beliefs and Anger

Your anger habit is fueled by negative beliefs. Negative beliefs are like the gasoline and oil that run a car. That is a strong statement, but stop and think about it. Would you have developed an anger habit if you hadn't believed anger was a good way to change how you feel?

You used anger and violence to hurt people. You hurt them physically or emotionally or both. You could not have continued hurting people if you hadn't believed it was okay. Think about it: Your beliefs are the foundation for your anger habit. Your beliefs are the concrete upon which your anger habit is built, and it is your beliefs that keep you stuck.

In order to heal from anger and rage, you must identify the beliefs you hold about anger that keep you stuck, and then you must change those beliefs. You must change your beliefs about the meaning of anger. You must give up the belief that anger means pleasure and, instead, adopt the belief that anger means pain. Changing your basic beliefs about anger will make it easier to stop your angry behavior, because ***beliefs cause your behavior.***

A Message from Manny

Hi. My name is Manny. I'm from Detroit. I have an anger habit. I really wanted to stop the violence. I didn't want to hurt people anymore, with my words or my actions. I was full of guilt. I wanted to change; I wanted to recover from my anger habit. But I kept tripping over my negative beliefs. I had so many negative beliefs when I started my recovery! And I didn't know how much they kept me stuck. I didn't even know I had a choice in the matter; I thought I'd been born with my beliefs. I thought they were like arms and legs. When I found out I could change my beliefs, that gave me a new sense of freedom. Finally, I learned how to identify my negative beliefs; then I learned how to get rid of them and adopt new ones that weren't so self-defeating. That's when I started making real progress in my recovery from anger and rage.

◆ **EXERCISE 1** What are beliefs?

_____

_____

_____

_____

_____

◆ **EXERCISE 2** What effect do beliefs have on your behavior?

_____

_____

_____

_____

_____

_____

_____

◆ **EXERCISE 3** What do your beliefs have to do with your anger habit?

_____

_____

_____

_____

_____

_____

_____

◆ **EXERCISE 4** How did you acquire your beliefs and why must you change them?

_____

_____

_____

_____

_____

_____

_____

◆ **EXERCISE 1** First, you must *identify your beliefs about anger that keep you stuck.* Look at the list of beliefs below. Some of them may be familiar. Circle the beliefs that you hold to be true.

Anger means power.

I inherited my anger, so I can't change my angry behavior.

If I stop using anger, people will take advantage of me.

What other beliefs do you hold about anger that keep you stuck? List at least five.

_____

_____

_____

_____

_____

◆ **EXERCISE 2** Now pick a negative belief from your list and *make a decision to change it.* Recognize the belief for what it is: a *limitation.* That negative belief stands in the way of permanently changing the behaviors that have caused harm to other people and to yourself. You could even plug the negative belief you want to change into the motivation script you learned in Chapter 5.

I have made a decision to change the following belief:

_____

_____

_____

_____

_____

_____

◆ **EXERCISE 3** Now think of a positive belief that you want to adopt to replace the negative one. You may have targeted the belief "anger means power" as the one you want to change. Now you might write down, "I can learn how to feel powerful without using anger and violence," as the new belief to take the place of the old negative belief.

Examples of beliefs that will help you change old patterns of anger and rage:

I can learn new ways to feel powerful without using anger and rage.

I can learn how to gain respect without using violence and intimidation.

Anger means personal pain and pain for my loved ones.

What is the new belief you want in place of the old negative belief?

_____

_____

_____

_____

_____

_____

_____

◆ **EXERCISE 4** Now list three things you've already lost because of the negative beliefs you hold about anger and rage. Examples: loss of freedom, loss of career advancement, loss of a love relationship.

What are three things you have lost due to your negative beliefs about anger?

_____

_____

_____

◆ **EXERCISE 5** Now write three potential future losses you will suffer if you continue to hold the negative belief. Examples: further jail or prison time, more lost career opportunities, further rejection by others.

What are three things you will lose in the future if you don't let go of the negative belief?

_____

_____

_____

◆ **EXERCISE 6** Write three specific benefits you know you'll gain by changing that negative belief. Examples: improved health, career advancement, exciting new relationships.

What are three ways you will benefit if you do change the belief?

_____

_____

_____

◆ **EXERCISE 7** Now recall the old negative belief that you want to change, and look at the losses you listed. Close your eyes and visualize the three losses you've already suffered, and get in touch with the pain. Look at the future losses you listed and visualize yourself experiencing those future losses. Exactly how does that make you feel? Spend at least three minutes on this step.

How do you feel about your past losses, and how will you feel in the future if you do not change that belief?

_____

_____

_____

_____

_____

_____

_____

◆ **EXERCISE 8** Now recall the new positive belief and look at the benefits list. Close your eyes and imagine the future benefits that will come when you replace that old negative belief with the new positive belief. Notice how that will make you feel. Spend at least three minutes on this step.

How will the benefits of changing that negative belief make you feel in the future?

_____

_____

_____

_____

_____

The best time to go through this process is just before you go to sleep at night. Repeat the process every night for a period of five to seven days. Then you can start another cycle using a different negative belief.

LESSON 3 ~ Acquire Positive Beliefs About Yourself, Others, and the World

Positive beliefs are beliefs that make you feel good about yourself, others, and the rest of the world. Positive beliefs are *positive statements*. Positive statements about yourself are called *affirmations*.

Positive Beliefs about Yourself

◆ **EXERCISE 1** Read the positive beliefs listed below. They are affirmations about yourself. Read them to yourself every morning before you start your day and each night just before you go to sleep.

I am a worthwhile person.

I deserve to be happy.

I deserve love.

I deserve respect.

I have a purpose.

◆ **EXERCISE 2** Make a list of other self-empowering positive beliefs or affirmations that will help you heal from addictive anger.

Other self-empowering positive beliefs or affirmations I want to acquire are

_____

_____

_____

_____

_____

_____

_____

If possible, tape-record your self-empowering beliefs and then listen to the tape several times a day.

Positive Beliefs About Others

It is important to hold positive beliefs about yourself, and it is equally important to hold positive beliefs about others.

◆ **EXERCISE 1** Read the positive beliefs about others listed below. Circle the beliefs you already hold.

Most people are basically good.

Most people are willing to help you when you need their help.

Most people can be trusted.

◆ **EXERCISE 2** List at least three other positive beliefs you hold about others.

_____

_____

_____

◆ **EXERCISE 3** List at least three positive beliefs you would like to hold about other people but that you don't hold right now.

_____

_____

_____

Positive Beliefs About the World

It is important to have positive beliefs about yourself and others, and you also need positive beliefs about the world. Negative beliefs about the world will keep you stuck in your anger habit.

◆ **EXERCISE 1** Look at the positive beliefs about the world listed below and circle the beliefs you already hold:

> The world is mostly a friendly place.
>
> The world has meaning.
>
> I am a meaningful part of the world.
>
> I have an important part to play in the world.

◆ **EXERCISE 2** List at least three other positive beliefs you would like to hold about the world.

_____

_____

_____

Beliefs About Death

The fear of death weighs on the minds of all human beings. But people with an anger problem often feel the weight of the fear of death more heavily. Intense fear of death may be one of the basic causes of your anger habit. Intense fear of any kind is a major anger trigger.

Intense fear of death is directly related to negative beliefs about death. Until you give up your negative beliefs about death, you will never be rid of the fear of death. Until the fear of death is put to rest, that intense negative feeling will always be a major anger trigger.

◆ **Negative Beliefs About Death**

◆ **EXERCISE 1** Look at the negative beliefs about death listed below. Do you hold any of these beliefs? Circle the negative beliefs you hold about death.

Death is the end. There is nothing after that.

Death is the final insult.

After the struggle, death is your reward.

Death is a time of punishment and pain.

Life has no purpose—death, even less of a purpose.

◆ **EXERCISE 2** Do you hold other negative beliefs about death? Write them down.

_____

_____

_____

_____

◆ **EXERCISE 3** How do your negative beliefs about death make you feel?

_____

_____

_____

_____

◆ **Positive Beliefs About Death**

◆ **EXERCISE 1** Look at the positive beliefs about death listed below. Circle the ones you now hold, if any.

Death is not the end; it leads to greater growth.

Death is a great resting time.

The soul survives the death of the body.

This life is a school. If I learn what I need to learn, I will go to a higher grade when I die.

◆ **EXERCISE 2** List at least three positive beliefs about death you would like to hold.

_____

_____

_____

_____

◆ **EXERCISE 3** How would positive beliefs about death make you feel?

_____

_____

_____

_____

_____

A Message from Walt

My name is Walt. My anger habit cost me more than I like to admit. I lost five years of my freedom. I lost my family; I almost lost my life. I'm still on parole, but I'm starting to get my act together.

I didn't know how much I feared death. Of course, I denied that I was afraid of death at all. I was a real tough guy, you see. But death was one of my major fears. I didn't dwell on it all the time, at least not consciously. But, once in a while, it would pop up to the surface. Then I'd find myself thinking about it, and it made me angry.

My belief was, you live a little while; you go through a lot of pain; maybe you cop a little happiness; then you die; and that was it. Period. No applause, no reward. They stick you in the ground to rot. You as a personality disappear forever like a puff of smoke in a windstorm; that's what I used to believe about death. No wonder I got angry every time thoughts of death came into my mind.

Finally, I saw how my negative beliefs about death were keeping me stuck in my anger habit, so I decided to change my beliefs about it. I didn't care whether my new beliefs about death were "right" or "wrong." I didn't care whether they were "true" or "false." I chose some new beliefs about death, positive beliefs that reduced my fear of death and made it manageable. It took a little while to get used to the new beliefs. When they started to feel "true," my feelings about death changed. My fear of death got less and less, and that had a positive effect on my ability to manage my anger.

14

Life Mission and Spirituality

You have decided to change your angry behavior. You have sorted out your values. You have decided to change old beliefs about anger that keep you stuck. Now you have come to the next important step in your recovery from your anger habit. You must now discover your personal mission and write it down.

In this lesson you will learn the importance of identifying your life mission. You will write down your personal mission statement, and you will learn how to use it to help you manage anger.

Also in the lesson, you will learn more about the importance of developing your spirituality so that you will be able to heal completely from chronic anger and rage.

∾ What Is Your Life Mission? ∾

Your mission is what you believe to be the meaning of your life. It is what you believe you were born to be and to do. It is what you believe to be the main reason that you are alive. Your life mission is what is left when everything else that you find important about your life has been stripped away from you.

A Message from Floyd

My name is Floyd. I'm from Atlanta, and I'm an anger addict. I had no idea I had a purpose, a life mission; in fact, I was sure I didn't have a purpose and that no one else had a purpose either. That was one of the reasons I was so angry all the time. To me, life was meaningless. Believing that, I couldn't make sense out of anything. Even good feelings didn't make sense to me, and I sure couldn't make sense out of the pain in my life. I was an atheist, and, of course, that didn't help; as an atheist I was sure nothing had a purpose. Nothing had meaning to me; I believed everything happened by chance, like a dice game. That was before I heard of Einstein and his famous statement. He said, "God doesn't play dice with us," or something close to that. I don't think I could have discovered my life mission if I hadn't first given up being an atheist; finally I did. Then I discovered my purpose. I discovered my mission and wrote it down. Then things started making sense; then I could make sense even out of the pain.

170

Your mission *must benefit others*. It must bring good into your life, and it must bring good into the lives of others.

It is useful to believe that you were born with a mission but have forgotten what it is. Now you must rediscover your mission. Rediscovering your mission will be difficult, because your mission is buried deep inside your subconscious mind. But you can resurrect it by pulling it back up into consciousness the way the sun pulls flowers up from the earth in springtime.

It is useful to think of your mission not as a choice, but as a *mandate*. It is something you *must* do.

> *People who lack conscious awareness of their mission and have lost many of the things they value are at high risk for losing the will to live.*

Your mission statement is potentially your most powerful tool. It could pull you out of the anger process when everything else fails, and it could help keep you out of the process more of the time. Remember the Niagara Falls metaphor from Chapter 6? Your mission statement will be a powerful anchor in the bottom of your boat. It will reach shore no matter how far you are from the bank.

The Story of Viktor Frankl

The story of Viktor Frankl is often used to illustrate the power of personal mission. Viktor Frankl was a Jewish psychiatrist who spent four years in a Nazi concentration camp. Conditions in the camp were horrible. The conditions in the camp were so horrible, in fact, that they were almost beyond the comprehension of anyone who hadn't actually gone through it. The ratio of survival in the camp was one in twenty; for every person who survived, nineteen others died.

The Nazis did everything they could to strip away Frankl's humanity. They starved him, beat him, and humiliated him unmercifully. But the Nazis could not break this courageous man, no matter what they did.

Allied soldiers liberated Frankl's camp at the end of the war. When they saw how horrible things had been, they were amazed to find Frankl and a few others still alive. The soldiers looked at the conditions of the camp. They saw the pathetic condition of the few survivors and could not believe their eyes. When the soldiers interviewed Frankl, they could see that Frankl had been treated no better than those who died. The soldiers asked Viktor Frankl how he managed to survive when so few others were able to. Frankl said, "I survived because I had a mission."

At first the soldiers did not understand. They asked for clarification. Frankl said, "I survived because I had a mission. My mission was, first, just to survive this camp, and then to tell the whole world what happened here, so that no one would ever have to go through anything like this again."

That was Frankl's personal mission statement, and that is what kept Frankl alive.

Frankl said he stayed focused on his mission, and that his mission made it possible to make sense out of what was happening to him. It made it possible to make sense even out of the pain.

Frankl said he used his mission to manage his feelings; he used it to fight against fear and despair. *He used his mission to control the anger and rage he felt at the hands of the Nazis.* He knew he couldn't do or say anything in anger to his captors; they would kill him if he did.

Frankl said most of the prisoners who died didn't have a mission. Therefore, they couldn't make sense out of the pain. Some of them did or said angry things to the Nazis, and the Nazis killed them. Other prisoners became so depressed they lost all hope; they just gave up and died. Many committed suicide.

After his release from the concentration camp, Viktor Frankl went on to develop a new form of therapy. He called it *logo therapy.* In Greek, "logo" means "meaning." Frankl believed that *people suffering from emotional or addictive disorders will experience spontaneous healing* once they became consciously aware of their life mission. Frankl taught that people who have a conscious sense of purpose and mission live longer, happier lives.

LESSON 1 ~ How to Discover Your Life Mission

Frankl did not know what his mission was before he went to the concentration camp; he may not even have known he had a mission. At first he couldn't make sense out of the pain he experienced in the camp any more than the other prisoners could. As conditions at the camp got worse, Frankl's condition got worse. His body and mind began to break down. He, too, began to lose hope. Then out of deep despair, Frankl asked himself a simple question: "What is the meaning of my life? What is my mission?" The answer was, "My mission is to survive this camp, and then tell the whole world what happened here, so no other human being will ever have to go through anything like this again."

You must ask the same question Frankl asked: "What is the meaning of my life?" The answer will be *your life mission.*

Why Should You Write Down Your Mission Statement?

You read Viktor Frankl's story on pages 171 and 172. You saw how he used his mission statement as a way to manage his feelings; you saw he was able to use his mission statement to manage his anger. Frankl focused his attention on his mission *all of the time.* He was always aware of it and could always remember it. He kept it always in his consciousness, so that he would not forget it.

The reason you are writing down your mission is so that you will remember it. You will forget it if you don't write it down. If you forget your life mission, you will be unable to use it to help yourself make sense out of what is happening in your life.

◆ **EXERCISE** Write your mission statement. The following are the ground rules:

1. Your mission statement should begin with your commitment to remain free from violence.

2. Your mission statement should be brief (twenty-five words or less).

3. Your mission statement should cause you to have strong positive feelings about yourself, other people, and the world.

4. Your mission statement should reflect your highest values.

5. Your mission statement must benefit other people as well as yourself.

6. Your mission statement should make you feel a sense of *urgency*. Reading it should make you feel that you *must* fulfill your mission.

The following are two examples of life mission statements that others have written:

"My life mission is to continue to recover from my anger habit and behave in a way that pulls out the best from myself and others."

"My life mission is to stay free of violence, and live each day as though it were my last, while listening to and serving others in a way that helps them be happy."

Pathways to Peace Founder's Mission Statement

Pathways to Peace founder Bill Fleeman spent a lot of time thinking about his mission statement before writing it down. It was not an easy task. When he finally got it down, he felt at the time that it was exactly as he wanted it to look and sound. He felt certain it would be the final version. About a year later, Bill found it necessary to rewrite it because he had continued to change and grow. He had to change his mission statement so that it would reflect the change and growth he had experienced. Another year went by, and Bill changed and grew a little more, so he had to change his mission statement again. The changes he made each time did not result in a completely different mission statement. The result of each change was an expansion of the original mission statement. Bill believes his mission statement will continue to change, at least in small ways, as he continues to change and grow and follow his personal pathway to peace.

Each morning before he starts his day, Bill recites his mission statement along with a prayer that's based, in part, on the Prayer of Saint Francis of Assisi. (Like Alcoholics Anonymous cofounder Bill W., Pathways to Peace founder Bill has borrowed from many different spiritual sources.) Here is his current mission statement. The prayer Bill uses is included in the section on spirituality, later in this chapter.

My life mission is to live violence-free and to inspire and empower as many other human beings as possible to find their pathway to peace, by providing them with the most effective tools and skills available with which to learn, to grow, to heal, to teach, and to inspire and empower others to find their pathway to peace.

Once you have completed your mission statement, make several copies. Keep a copy of your mission statement in your pocket or purse. Keep a copy of your mission statement next to your favorite chair; tape a copy to the bathroom mirror. Read your mission statement at least once in the morning and once at night. Read it every time an anger trigger occurs. If possible, record your mission statement on audiotape. Listen to the tape one or more times a day.

Write your mission statement on the following page. Use pencil, so you can erase, and take your time. This is a very important part of the healing process, so take it seriously. You will have to write more than one draft. You may have to write three or even more drafts before your mission statement is really complete.

My life mission is to remain violence-free and . . .

_____

_____

_____

_____

_____

_____

_____

LESSON 2 ~ Mission Support

You have discovered your mission and have written it down; now you must think about mission support. Every mission requires support. Your mission support is made of *positive feelings*. In order to stay on your mission, you must maintain a positive emotional state. You must feel good feelings, consistently. Of course you can't feel good all of the time, but in order to stay on your mission, you must feel good most of the time. Positive feelings help you stay on course; they help you keep moving in the direction of your mission. Negative feelings will send you off course, away from your mission. Anger is a negative feeling, so anger will knock you off course. Confidence is a positive feeling, so confidence will keep you on course.

◆ **EXERCISE** You must make a list of the positive feelings that represent your mission support. You may refer to your values list from Chapter 12. Your valued feelings are the kind of positive feelings you will need to include on your mission support list. If you did a thorough job of writing your values list, you can use the valued feelings you wrote down to get started on your mission support list. Write your positive feelings on the form provided on the next page. Try to list at least twenty positive feelings on your mission support list. Remember: These are the feelings that will help you stay focused on your life mission.

Mission Support

1. _____

2. _____

3. _____

4. _____

5. _____

6. _____

7. _____

8. _____

9. _____

10. _____

11. _____

12. _____

13. _____

14. _____

15. _____

16. _____

17. _____

18. _____

19. _____

20. _____

A Message from Bill

When I discovered my mission, things happened that made me aware of its power. One very dramatic thing happened. It was when I was working as a counselor. I woke up feeling sick one morning. I was feverish and had a headache; I felt bad all over. Thinking I might feel better later, I went to work anyway. Later I felt worse instead of better and decided to go home early. On my way out, a client stopped me in the hallway. He said he was depressed and needed to talk; he said he was afraid he was going to have an anger outburst if he didn't talk to somebody.

At first I thought, "Why me?" I was about to tell him to go talk to somebody else, then changed my mind. A small voice inside my mind whispered, "Hey, Bill! What are you doing here on the earth? What is your purpose? How come you're taking up space on this planet?" I unlocked my office and the depressed client and I went in and sat down. I really didn't feel like counseling. But I listened to the client's story and gave him some feedback. After about forty-five minutes, I ended the session.

As he walked out the door, the client said he felt a little better after talking to me. As I cleared my desk and prepared to leave, I made a remarkable discovery: All my symptoms were gone! I felt my forehead; it was cool to the touch. My fever was gone! So was my headache. I no longer felt ill. The client had said he felt a little better; I felt a lot better! And I felt great the rest of the day and night.

Why had my symptoms disappeared, I wondered? What happened to my fever and headache? At first it puzzled me, but then I figured it out. My personal mission was to help people. Though I was ill and didn't, at first, want to stop on my way out the door and meet with the client, my personal mission popped into my conscious mind. Becoming consciously aware of my life mission caused me to set aside my desire to go home and, instead, spend at least a little time with the client who had sought my help.

During the counseling session, I became totally focused on helping him. All my mental and emotional energy was focused on that goal. My mission called on every other part of my being to help, including the biological part. Even my immune system made an all-out effort. It removed all of my symptoms so that I would have the physical energy I needed to get through the session.

LESSON 3 ~ Spirituality

In Chapter 3, you learned that spirituality is defined as a feeling that you are "connected to other people; to the universe; and to the God of your understanding, whatever that may mean to you in your overall view of the world."

In order to change your angry behavior and be happy, you must completely change and grow at every part of your whole self. If you don't change and grow at all parts of your whole self, you will not be happy. If you are not happy, you will be unable to keep your behavior changed. You will relapse back into angry, violent behavior. That means you must take a close and serious look at your spiritual part. It means you must adopt a spiritual belief system that supports your new violence-free lifestyle.

To be happy means to be contented, or joyous, or serene. It can also mean to be blissful, satisfied, or merry. There are many other words that describe what it means to be happy. The word you choose to describe what happiness means to you will depend on your own unique personal history and experience.

In Chapter 3, you learned about the eight parts of the self. All of the eight parts of the self, together, determine whether you will be happy or unhappy as you continue to work on your anger and continue to change and grow. But the primary determinant is the very highest level, that is, the level of spirituality. The quality of your spirituality will largely determine the quality of all of the other parts of your whole self.

People who are spiritually fit will have a positive personal mission; will possess useful, empowering beliefs; will have uplifting values and worthwhile goals; will develop good anger management skills; will exhibit nonviolent behavior; will choose a supportive environment; and will feel physically and emotionally well. People who are spiritually healthy have more choices in general, and naturally choose people, places, and things that reinforce their change and growth.

Although some spiritually focused people may experience ongoing physical and emotional pain, even very intense pain on a daily basis, they are able to deal with it more effectively and develop skills that allow them to move out of pain very quickly. In general, people who focus on their spiritual part in a balanced way experience less conflict in their lives, and less pain.

People who have never had a problem with anger or have never been addicted to anger are usually those who have a well-developed spiritual life. People in the Pathways to Peace program who consistently pay attention to their spiritual part are much more likely to enjoy contented recovery. In fact, chronic anger and rage are often the inevitable responses to the feelings of powerlessness that arise when a person fails to find meaning at the spiritual level.

It is interesting to note that people who abuse chemicals are often trying to experience a feeling of connectedness to others, to the universe, and to some abstract "something" outside of themselves. For alcoholics and drug addicts, use of alcohol and other drugs might be a "spiritual search." Also, they use alcohol and other drugs in a vain attempt to kill the emotional pain that inevitably results from feeling totally disconnected and alone. Remember Bill's story? He was addicted to anger and rage, as well as to alcohol and other drugs. It has long been known that the main reason for the great success of twelve-step programs is that they are spiritually based.

The spiritual part of the whole self is related to all of the parts but is related most closely to the higher levels. It is more closely related to mission than to any other part of the whole self, which is why spirituality is included in this chapter along with personal mission.

A well-defined spiritual focus causes your brain to organize all of your resources differently. It gives you a totally different personal identity. It encourages you to adopt different beliefs, reorder your values, and set goals that you would not otherwise set, or even entertain. It encourages you to develop better skills, and makes it easier to change your behavior. As you learned in Chapter 3, your spirituality even affects your physical and emotional health.

What Kind of Spirituality Should You Adopt?

Clearly, Pathways to Peace suggests that recovery from chronic anger and rage must include spirituality as part of the process. But it is not the job of Pathways to Peace to choose your spiritual path. It is up to you to find or develop a spirituality that serves you best. Pathways to Peace makes only one suggestion: Whatever spiritual approach you decide to adopt should be based on nonviolent principles. Otherwise, it will work against you, instead of supporting your new nonviolent lifestyle. Bear this in mind that whatever spiritual philosophy or religion you choose as a way to experience and express your spirituality will be closely connected to your mission, yet will take you even beyond it.

The way people get in touch with their spirituality differs from culture to culture and from individual to individual. All cultures have rituals that help people get in touch with their spirituality. In some cultures, people learn spiritual rituals from the village shaman. In other cultures, such as Judeo-Christian cultures, people learn their rituals from ministers, priests, rabbis, or other spiritual leaders. In most cultures, people come together periodically to share their rituals with one another. They attend festivals and go to churches, temples, or other places of worship. Always, the desired goal is to experience a feeling of connectedness to other people, to the universe, and to the God of their understanding.

Find Your Spiritual Path

You may already have been on a spiritual path, even before you found Pathways to Peace, that serves you well. If that is the case, then you will only need to continue on that particular spiritual path. If you have not yet found a satisfying spiritual path, then you will want to focus on finding or developing one.

One way to begin the process of developing a healthy spirituality is through reading. Go to the library or onto the Internet and read about spirituality. Another way to begin your spiritual exploration is by attending services at various places of worship. You could take a class on comparative religion at your local college. You could join a discussion group. There are many others ways to acquire information about spirituality. Be creative. Above all, you are strongly urged not to omit this part of the recovery process. Unless you pay attention to this part of the recovery process—the highest, most powerful, and most sacred part of your whole self—you will be unable to heal completely from your anger problem.

After you have adopted a spiritual philosophy that supports your recovery from your anger problem, you will need some kind of ritual to help you maintain conscious awareness of this important part of your whole self. In order to maintain his awareness of the importance of spirituality, the founder of Pathways to Peace chose to use a daily ritual of prayer. First, Bill recites his mission statement, and then he recites the following prayer:

> *God, Great Spirit, this is my mission, my purpose. I believe it is Your will for me. In order to stay on my path and do Your will, I am entirely ready to have You remove all of my defects of character that stand in the way of my doing Your will and that block my path. I therefore ask You to please remove now all of my angry, resentful, anxious, fearful, frustrated, and impatient thoughts, words, and actions, and to make of me instead a channel of your peace: that where there is hatred, I may bring love; that where there is wrong, the spirit of forgiveness; that where there is doubt, faith; that where there is discord, harmony; that where there is error, truth; that where there is despair, hope; that where there are shadows, light; that where there is sadness, joy. God grant that I may seek rather to comfort than to be comforted; to understand than to be understood; to love than to be loved; for it is by self-forgetting that one finds; it is by forgiving that one is forgiven; it is by dying to self that one awakens to eternal life."*

◆ **EXERCISE** Pathways to Peace founder Bill chose prayer to help himself stay consciously aware of the importance of the spiritual part of his recovery from chronic anger and rage. What ritual will you use?

15

Goals

You have a mission, and now you need meaningful goals. Goals let you know you are still on your mission.

Your main goal must be to maintain your behavior change. Maintaining your new violence-free lifestyle must continue to be your most important goal. You have many good reasons to maintain that goal: to keep your family intact, to maintain your self-respect, to fulfill your purpose.

Goals keep you focused on your mission. A goal is based on a need. For example, you may need a new pair of shoes, but until you focus on a new pair of shoes as a goal and put a plan of action into place, you will never get them. You will sit in your chair needing a new pair of shoes, and the shoes will sit on the shelf needing a buyer. Nothing will ever come of it. Changing your angry behavior has to be a goal, not just a need.

You have decided *not* to use anger to feel important and powerful and you have decided to work a program to avoid falling back into angry behavior. Staying rage-free must always be your number one goal. Your main goal should be to continue your recovery from your anger problem. But now you must set other goals, too. You must set goals around each of the eight steps of recovery. The goals you set in each of the eight steps will lead you to your main goal.

LESSON 1 ~ What Is a Goal?

A goal is not a wish or a dream—wishes and dreams are vague ideas about the future. A goal is a clearly defined, reachable, future destination. It is the end of a carefully designed plan.

Goals Have Six Elements

A goal

1. must be a clear statement about something you really want

2. must be positive and move you forward in your recovery and toward your mission

3. must be reachable and clearly specified in writing

4. must include a timeframe

5. must include a method that has immediate action steps

6. must include a way to measure progress

If a goal does not include these six elements, it is not a goal. It is a wish or a dream.

Steps to Successful Goal Setting and Achievement

Goal setting and goal achievement is a four-step process. You must make four decisions and then follow through on them.

◆ STEP 1 | Define the Goal

First you need to decide on a reachable goal. Ask yourself if the goal you want to set is reachable; if in doubt, ask others for their opinion. You must be specific. Ask yourself exactly what you want to accomplish. Let's say you decide you want to lose weight, because being at a healthier weight will be good for the biological part of you (your body). Saying that your goal is simply to lose weight is not specific enough; you must *specify* the amount of weight you want to lose. Let's say you decide to lose twenty pounds; twenty pounds is *specific*.

◆ STEP 2 | Set the Timeframe

Now you must decide exactly when you want to lose the twenty pounds. Let's say you decide on a six-month timeframe. Let's assume today is the first of January. If today is the first of January, then the first of June should be your target date, exactly six months from today.

◆ STEP 3 | Plan the Method

Next you must decide on a method and then take immediate action. Let's say you decide to do the following:

A. to reduce your intake of carbohydrates below one hundred grams per day and increase your protein to one hundred grams per day (the figures given are used only as examples)

B. to exercise three times a week for forty-five minutes

C. (this is the action step; actually, it is a series of action steps)

    1. to go to the store and buy a carbohydrate gram counter

    2. to use the carbohydrate gram counter as a guide for meal preparation

    3. to join a health club and complete your first workout

Now you must decide how to measure your progress. If you don't know whether or not you are moving toward your goal, you will lose interest. Then you will give up; if you give up, you will fail.

You must think of the best way to measure your progress. You could keep track of what notch you are using on your belt; that's one way to see if you are losing weight and moving toward your goal. But you could lose inches by exercising and still not lose weight, so that may not be a good way to measure your progress. You could use a scale. You could weigh yourself the day you start your program, and then weigh yourself once a week and see exactly how many pounds you lost. A scale would give you an accurate way of measuring your progress. There would be no guesswork.

Now you can write a clear, specific goal statement that would look and sound like this:

"I will lose twenty pounds by the first of June, six months from today. I will reduce my intake of carbohydrates below one hundred grams per day and increase my protein to one hundred grams. I will exercise for forty-five minutes three times a week. I will weigh myself once a week to check my progress."

Now you have a clearly defined destination. You have a plan, and you have taken action. Now you have a real goal, not just a vague wish or dream for the future. Here is an outline of the steps:

1. Set a specific goal and write it down.

2. Choose a specific timeframe.

3. Determine a method and take immediate action.

4. Find a way to measure your progress.

A Message from Bill

In a previous message I said I didn't have any goals. I didn't. Now I have goals. Maintaining my recovery from my anger habit (and from all my other addictions) is still my main goal, but I have other goals, too. I set goals around all eight parts of my whole self. My goals move me ahead on all eight recovery steps.

Goals have to do with the future. But when I set a goal, I don't go and live there with it in the future. I think of the goal I want to set, then I set it; that means I write it down. Then I focus back on the here-and-now.

I have to have something to look forward to, something to plan for, but it has to be meaningful. So when I set a goal, it has to connect with one of my higher values; it has to satisfy my recovery mission and move me forward. If it doesn't connect to a higher value, I'll lose interest. I never set a goal that conflicts with my values. When I've done that in the past, I usually failed, or if I attained my goal, I felt disappointed instead of glad.

You can apply this goal-setting and goal-achievement formula to any goal. If the goal is reachable, you will succeed.

◆ **EXERCISE 1** What is a goal?

_____

_____

_____

_____

_____

_____

◆ **EXERCISE 2** What are the six elements of a goal? Feel free to refer back to the text if you cannot recall the six elements.

_____

_____

_____

_____

_____

_____

◆ **EXERCISE 3** Name the four steps to successful goal setting and goal achievement. Feel free to refer back to the text if you cannot recall the four steps.

_____

_____

_____

_____

Start by thinking about the Eight Parts of the Whole Self, which are explained in Chapter 3. The Eight Parts of the Whole Self are the framework for the recovery goals you must set. Your goals should lead to improvement in each part.

1. **Biological (Physical) Goals**—goals for the health of your body

2. **Environment Goals**—goals about where you will live and whom you will live with

3. **Behavior Goals**—goals about your actions and words

4. **Skill Goals**—goals about learning new things and acquiring new tools

5. **Value Goals**—goals about expanding your values

6. **Belief Goals**—goals about letting go of limiting beliefs and adopting new beliefs that support your recovery

7. **Mission Goals**—goals that move you toward your mission

8. **Spiritual Goals**—goals that help you feel connected to others, to the world, and to the God of your understanding

Look at Part One of the Whole Self, the biological (physical) self. Ask yourself, "What must I do to improve the biological (physical) part of my self?" Using the word "must" instead of "could" makes it more likely you will follow through. Then list two to three things you must do to improve that part of your self.

Then go on to the next part. Ask yourself, "What must I do to improve the environmental part of my self?" Then write down two to three things you must do to improve that part. Follow this procedure in each of the Eight Parts of the Whole Self. Two examples are given below for each part, to get you started. Your job is to come up with three more goals for each part. Spend at least five minutes on each part.

It is important to understand the nature of goals and the power that goals have in your life. Goals are things you want to move toward that will lead to the feelings you want and deserve. Goals help you satisfy your *positive values*. You want to stay *happily* free of excessive anger, so you must be goal-oriented. Goals keep you on track and move you toward your mission.

◆ **EXERCISE** Two examples of each type of goal are given below; in the blank lines, write two or three of your own.

Biological (Physical) Goals

1. Stop smoking by my next birthday.

2. Attain my ideal weight (be specific about what it is) by June 1st.

3. _____

4. _____

5. _____

Behavior Goals

1. Notice when I am speaking too loudly and immediately reduce the volume.

2. Become aware when I'm breathing too rapidly due to stress, and slow down my breathing.

3. _____

4. _____

5. _____

Environment Goals

1. Listen to relaxing music fifteen minutes a day over the next three months.

2. Make two new nonviolent friends within two weeks of now.

3. _____

4. _____

5. _____

Skills Goals

1. Learn how to relax under stress in less than two minutes.

2. Teach relaxation skills to three other people in the next thirty days.

3. _____

4. _____

5. _____

Values Goals

1. Read my values list every morning before I leave the house.

2. Discover ten more of my valued feelings within two weeks.

3. _____

4. _____

5. _____

Beliefs Goals

1. Identify two more of my negative beliefs and change them within thirty days.

2. Adopt two positive beliefs about other people by the end of this month.

3. _____

4. _____

5. _____

Mission Goals

1. Memorize my mission statement within one week.

2. Recite my mission statement once at night and once in the morning, starting tonight.

3. _____

4. _____

5. _____

Spiritual Goals

1. Read from spiritual literature once at night and once in the morning, starting today.

2. Visit two different churches within the next thirty days.

3. _____

4. _____

5. _____

Move Toward Your Goals

In the past you were motivated to use anger and rage to move away from painful feelings such as anxiety or frustration. As you start your recovery from your anger habit, you will sometimes find yourself without resources to move away from painful things and conditions. Goals will help you move toward positive feelings and things. The reason you decided to change your behavior in the first place may have been to avoid further pain and negative results; now you will have positive goals to move toward that will help you feel better about yourself and the world.

You have taken the time to set some goals, so now you can begin to move toward something meaningful. Now you can spend more time and energy moving toward the conditions and things you want in your life. This does not mean you should completely forget about the pain of the past. It does not mean you should become complacent. You must stay aware of the pain and chaos that will occur if you fall back into destructive behavior.

But you must learn to focus more time and energy on your goals. Achieving goals will help you go beyond the mere avoidance of painful results. Your goals will help you find the kind of fulfilled and happy life that you deserve.

As soon as you set a goal, things start happening. Your brain automatically gathers its resources to get you to your goal. *Your brain will take you anywhere you want to go. But you have to tell it exactly where you want to go. You have to put it in writing.*

Goals will keep you moving toward your mission. Your mission will let you know that recovery is more than the mere *absence of violence,* more than the *absence of pain.* True recovery is the *presence of purpose, meaning, and happiness.*

◆ How to Succeed

1. Visualize success.

2. Hold on to the feeling.

3. Visualize your present goal.

4. Take an action step—now!

5. Repeat.

LESSON 3 ~ Set a Goal to Stop the Use of Rage and Violence

You want to stop using anger and rage to change how you feel, and you want to stay stopped; therefore, you must make it a goal. And you must write it down. Your goal statement must include the benefits of stopping as well as the negative results of continuing the behavior. When writing your goal statement, use language that makes you feel you have no choice but to stop using anger and rage immediately.

◆ EXERCISE

1. Write down a clear, concise goal statement (less than twenty words), including a timeframe. Example: "I will stop using anger, rage, and violence to feel powerful over people, places, and things, beginning this date: _____."

_____

_____

_____

_____

_____

2. Write down three specific benefits you believe will make the effort worthwhile. Examples: more freedom in my career, improved cardiovascular health, improved relationship with my significant other.

Benefits:

_____

_____

_____

_____

3. Write down three specific losses that you know will cause you severe emotional pain if you don't stop using anger to change how you feel. Examples: I will lose out on career advancement because my boss can't stand my angry behavior; I may become a heart patient or die a premature death; I may lose my present relationship or miss out on developing a relationship with someone I really care about; I may go to prison (again).

Losses:

_____

_____

_____

_____

4. Look at the losses you listed. Close your eyes and visualize experiencing the losses. Get in touch with the pain. Example: imagine yourself in prison, separated from your loved ones. Spend one to two minutes doing this step.

5. Look at the benefits list. Close your eyes and visualize experiencing the benefits. See an image of yourself responding differently to old triggers and enjoying each of the benefits. Spend three to five minutes doing this step.

6. Review Step 4 once daily in the morning and follow it immediately with Step 5. Repeat Steps 4 and 5 again in the evening before you go to sleep.

16

Forgiveness

Forgiveness is the final step in the recovery process.

The word *forgiveness* means to *cease to resent;* it means to *pardon* or *release.* Some of the things that were done to you may have been horrible beyond words; some of the things you have done to others may have been as bad. But in order to heal from your anger habit, you must forgive those who harmed you and you must forgive yourself. Unless you forgive, the pain of the past won't go away.

Unless you forgive others, your feelings of humiliation and resentment will continue. Unless you forgive yourself, your feelings of guilt and shame will keep you trapped. For you, these negative feelings are triggers for anger and rage. They will rise up from the past and trigger your anger; in the terms of the Niagara Falls metaphor, they will plunge you into the river and over the Falls.

Forgiving others releases you from the deep resentment that keeps you stuck; forgiving yourself releases you from toxic guilt and shame. Guilt and shame are toxic for you because you have an anger problem. Guilt and shame are anger triggers and they will keep you stuck in the river.

Unless you forgive, the memories of what has been done to you
and what you have done to others will continue to haunt you.

Once you forgive, you will be amazed. You will know what the caged bird feels when it is released, and why it sings. You will move with enormous energy toward your goals. You will discover the joy that can be found in service to others. You will make a giant leap toward your mission. You will know the meaning of serenity. You will feel connected to others, to the world, and to the God of your understanding as never before. You will feel transformed.

But forgiving is not an easy thing to do. The hardest part of forgiveness is getting past your negative beliefs about forgiveness. Look at the examples of negative beliefs about forgiveness that are listed below.

Examples of Negative Beliefs about Forgiveness

Forgiveness means wimping out; it means allowing people to walk all over me.

I could never forgive those who caused me so much pain.

Those who hurt me don't deserve to be forgiven.

I don't deserve to be forgiven.

I can't forgive myself.

◆ **EXERCISE 1** What does the word *forgiveness* mean?

_____

_____

_____

_____

_____

◆ **EXERCISE 2** Why is forgiveness so important?

_____

_____

_____

_____

_____

_____

_____

◆ **EXERCISE 3** This exercise will help prepare you to forgive others and yourself. Review the belief change skill you learned in Chapter 13 on beliefs. Think of at least two positive beliefs about forgiveness that will help you begin to forgive.

LESSON 2 ~ Forgive Others

You must forgive those who harmed you in the past, no matter how much you may have suffered as a result of what was done to you. No matter how great the pain, no matter how deep the scars on your body or in your mind, you must find it in your heart to forgive those who harmed you. You must not hold on to your resentment and hate. If you refuse to forgive, you will fall back into your old behaviors. You will not heal unless you forgive.

In order to forgive, you do not have to *forget*. In fact, it is not even possible to forget. You can repress, but you cannot forget what has been done to you.

When you forgive, you will stop thinking about those who harmed you; you will stop thinking about what they did. Once you forgive, your overall tension level will decrease and you will feel less anxiety as you go about your daily life. You will have fewer anger outbursts. You will have more positive energy to deal with stressors that occur every day in the here and now.

As you forgive all those who have harmed you, remember this: You are not forgiving them for *their* good, you are forgiving them for *your own* good.

◆ **EXERCISE 1** Make a list of people who have harmed you. Limit your list to those who have *greatly* harmed you; limit it to those about whom you have strong feelings of anger. Briefly state what the person did to you and how it made you feel. The first entry is an example.

Name: My father.

What the person did: He came home drunk and beat me up.

How it made me feel: I felt unloved.

Name: _____

What the person did: _____

How it made me feel: _____

Name: _____

What the person did: _____

How it made me feel: _____

Name: _____

What the person did: _____

How it made me feel: _____

Name: _____

What the person did: _____

How it made me feel: _____

Name: _____

What the person did: _____

How it made me feel: _____

Name: _____

What the person did: _____

How it made me feel: _____

◆ **EXERCISE 2** Find a quiet place to sit. Read the statement below to yourself, filling in the blank with the name of the person you have made a decision to forgive. There may be more than one person you need to forgive, but start with one person. When you feel you have really forgiven that person, write the next person's name in the blank.

> *"I forgive you, _____, not because I have gotten over what you did to me. I forgive you not just because I want to be free of the pain you inflicted on me. I forgive you so that I may be free of the anger that pain has caused in my life, which contributed to the pain I have caused others. I forgive you so that I may break the cycle of anger and hate and violence. I forgive you so that I may not use what you did to me as an excuse to hurt others ever again."*

After you have completed the exercise, call your Pathways to Peace mentor or a Pathways to Peace friend and tell them what you have just accomplished. Share it, in a general way, at your next Pathways to Peace meeting. Open yourself up to feedback from the group.

You may need to repeat this exercise more than once. You may need to repeat it many times before you *feel* you have truly forgiven those who harmed you. Repeat the exercise once or twice a day, until you really *feel* you have forgiven.

LESSON 3 ~ Forgive Yourself

In order to stop the abuse and violence once and for all, you must forgive others. But you must also forgive yourself. If you fail to take whatever steps may be required to fully accomplish self-forgiveness, you'll stop short of your main goal. It would be like climbing a mountain, only to stop and hide in the shadows of a cave just a few yards from the summit and deprive yourself of the spectacular view that would be your glorious reward. You have come this far; you have struggled as few human beings have struggled. You deserve to win the prize. So don't stop now—go all the way to the mountaintop.

As in the previous exercise on forgiving others, find a quiet place to sit. Read the statement below to yourself. When you have finished, share what you have accomplished with your Pathways to Peace mentor or with a Pathways to Peace friend.

◆ **EXERCISE 1** Make a list of people you have harmed because of your anger. Next to each name, briefly state what you did to the person. You can refer back to Chapter 4 and the list you made of people you have harmed, and include those names on your list. If you feel you have done major harm to more than five people, you can add them on a separate sheet of paper. The first entry is an example.

Name: John (my son)

What I did: I screamed at John and called him stupid.

The result: John broke down and cried.

Name: _____

What I did: _____

The result: _____

Name: _____

What I did: _____

The result: _____

Name: _____

What I did: _____

The result: _____

Name: _____

What I did: _____

The result: _____

Name: _____

What I did: _____

The result: _____

Name: _____

What I did: _____

The result: _____

◆ **EXERCISE 2** Find a quiet place to sit, then read the statement below to yourself.

"I forgive myself for hurting _____, *not because I feel what I did is excusable in any way, or that I do not deserve the consequences I suffered or may suffer in the future because of my actions. I forgive myself so that I may heal from the over-whelming guilt I have felt, which would continue to trigger anger and rage in me in the future, against others as well as myself."*

Repeat this exercise at least once a day until you really *feel* you have forgiven yourself.

～ Conclusion ～

In Chapter 4 you were asked to become willing to forgive. You did some exercises about making amends to people you had hurt. Review the work you did. Are there some loose ends you need to tie up? Do you need to follow up your forgiveness exercise with some more amends work? If so, now is the time.

Forgiveness is an ongoing process. Be patient with yourself. If the anger and hurt keep coming back, you know you're not done. Work at it. You'll know when you're done, because the pain will go away.

A Message from Anne

My name is Anne. I now live in San Diego. I have an anger habit. In the past, I used anger like a drug. I know how important forgiveness is.

I was thirty before I began my recovery. I was a hurtin' unit, as they say; I was full of rage. My father had abused me, if you know what I mean. I was in kindergarten when he did it the first time. My mother found out when I was twelve. She wanted to kill him; instead, she took me away. I was angry at my father for what he did; I was angry with my mother for taking me away. I was so confused! I took my anger out on everybody. Finally, I saw I was addicted to anger. Fortunately, I also saw that I could change my behavior. I changed some of my behavior fast. But I wanted to be happy, not just nonviolent, so I knew I had to forgive. I forgave my father in an un-sent letter, because he was dead by then; I forgave my mother face-to-face; finally, I forgave myself. Forgiving myself was the hardest part. Having forgiven others as well as myself, I started growing fast—I mean fast!

Sometimes my life is still no bed of roses. But there are moments, now, that are wonderful! Most of the time I feel good about myself, and most of the time I feel good about other people. That's totally different than it used to be.

Self-Contract

When you began this workbook, you signed a fourteen-point self-agreement. You have now completed this workbook, but completing this workbook is only the beginning. Now you must continue to apply what you have learned.

Now it is time to sign a self-contract. A self-contract is stronger than an agreement. An agreement indicates you will try to fulfill the points of the agreement to the best of your ability at the time it is written; a contract is a promise, a *total commitment*. A self-contract means you won't just try; it means you will fulfill all the points. Period.

Now you understand the nature of anger and rage. Now you know how to change your angry behavior and stop the violence. Now you have no excuses. Now you are ready for a self-contract.

Look at the self-contract below. Do not enter into it lightly. If you violate your self-contract, you violate yourself, no one else. You will want to have someone you like and admire witness your signature.

I, _____, am now totally committed to living a

violence-free life from this day on, as of this date, _____

1. I have admitted I have a problem with anger. I admit I have harmed others, property, and myself. I have apologized and made restitution wherever possible.

2. I now fully accept personal responsibility for the results of my actions. I have made a firm decision to stop my harmful behavior.

3. I once used threats and verbal or physical violence to feel powerful. Now I understand I am never justified in using violence, unless it is a matter of life or death.

4. I have learned and will continue to learn ways to feel personal power that do not violate other people's right to feel safe in their person and property.

5. I am totally committed to treating all people with respect and dignity.

6. I believe I have the ability to change and grow.

7. I believe I have a purpose that goes beyond my own selfish desires.

8. I have forgiven those who harmed me. And I have forgiven myself for the harm I have done others.

9. I am committed to helping others recover from anger, rage, and violence.

10. I am committed to continuing my path of emotional, mental, and spiritual growth.

11. I am committed to joining a Pathways to Peace group to help me keep the momentum going.

12. I understand that violating this contract is a violation of myself.

Signature: _____   Witness: _____

Conclusion

Congratulations! You have just completed a major task. The workbook you have just finished required a lot of study and effort. But your job has just begun. Now you must maintain the changes you have made, and you must make yet more changes. You must continue to grow and continue to work all of the eight steps of your recovery.

You may already be a member of Pathways to Peace; if not, you are strongly encouraged to join a Pathways to Peace group in your area as soon as possible. You will need the influence of a Pathways to Peace group to help you keep the momentum going. You will need a Pathways to Peace mentor to help you along.

A Message from Bill

I met a man a long time ago whose name was Clyde. I met Clyde at an AA meeting. I had just lost a good job because of my anger and was telling the group how it was my boss's fault, not mine. I said my boss had provoked me and that I would get him for it.

That's when Clyde interrupted me. Clyde was born on a Chippewa Indian reservation in Upper Michigan but now lived in Detroit. Clyde was a big guy. He was 6' 4" and weighed 275. He didn't have much fat, either. So when Clyde interrupted, you couldn't just dismiss him. He looked straight at me and said, "My name is Clyde, and I'm an alcoholic. I'm addicted to anger, too." Then he said, "Look at my face." I looked at his face. He said, "What do you see there?" Clyde's face had scars everywhere. I told him what I saw.

Clyde said, "Yeah, I've got a lot of scars, from broken beer bottles and knives. I've got gunshot scars, too, but you can't see them—they're under my shirt. I used to be in denial about my drinking; then I got sober. Then I was in denial about my anger habit. Then I got in a fight one night with a drunk. I was sober, but I was angry, real angry. That guy gave me my last scar. This one." Clyde pointed to a deep scar that ran the length of his cheekbone. "I hit that guy hard. He'd left himself wide open. When I hit him, he fell and hit his head on the curb. His head broke like an egg; he died instantly. I didn't mean to kill him, but he died. They sent me to prison. It wasn't my first time in prison, but it was my longest—ten years."

Clyde leaned toward me. The muscles in his neck stood out like ropes. "I was playing semi-pro football when that happened. The Detroit Lions and other pro teams were looking at me." Clyde stopped to clear his throat. "Now I'm too old," he said. Clyde leaned closer. His eyes were like two sharp, black coals.

"If you don't learn how to manage your anger," Clyde said, "someone else will do it for you. You'll be the policeman's slave. You'll be the dope man's slave. You'll be everybody's slave." Then Clyde got up and walked out.

Appendix 1

The Pathways to Peace
Self-Help Program

✍ Overview: What Is Pathways to Peace? ✍

Pathways to Peace, founded in 1998 and receiving official tax-exempt status as a not-for-profit corporation in 2000, is a self-help program for people who have problems with anger and rage. Members meet in groups once a week or more to help each other understand anger and rage and to help each other stop using violent behavior. Group members help each other by sharing their stories and by showing each other they can change.

There are Pathways to Peace groups scattered throughout the United States and membership is growing rapidly throughout the country.

Anyone with an anger problem may join us. Having a problem with anger is the only requirement. Pathways to Peace is free.

✍ The Purpose of Pathways to Peace ✍

The purpose of Pathways to Peace is clear: to help people stop their violent behavior; to help people discover and pursue their highest values; to help people reach their goals; and to help people learn how to grow, to heal, and to help others who have a problem with anger and rage so that they may find their pathway to peace.

✍ What Types of People Join Pathways to Peace? ✍

Pathways to Peace members come from all walks of life, from all over the world. They are men and women of every race and religion and are of all ages. Some are married, some are divorced or separated, and some have never been married. Some Pathways to Peace members have been in prison because of anger. Some members are told by the court they must attend Pathways to Peace; some are encouraged by others to attend. But most members attend Pathways to Peace on their own. They came to Pathways to Peace because they felt guilty and ashamed, and because they lost things they valued. Some members lost their wives or husbands, some lost their children, some lost their jobs, some lost their freedom.

All Pathways to Peace members have problems due to anger. All have harmed others, all are trying to change, all are trying to put the past behind and create a better future for themselves.

Principle 1

We admitted we have a problem with anger and have harmed people, property, and ourselves. Whenever possible, we make amends or restitution.

This is the first step to recovery. We wanted to change our angry behavior and stop the violence. First, we admitted we have a problem with anger. We admitted we had harmed others; we admitted we had harmed property; we admitted we had harmed ourselves. It was not easy. Most of us have felt the sting of guilt and shame, and have often tried to escape those painful feelings by denying the harm we caused. We thought admitting our problem would only add to our feelings of low self-worth. But we took this crucial first step; otherwise, we could not have changed.

Principle 2

We accepted responsibility for our actions and decided to stop our harmful behavior. We became willing to forgive those who harmed us, and to forgive ourselves for the harm we caused others.

This, too, was a difficult principle. But we found we had to take this step. The guilt and shame we suffered because of our actions sometimes took us to the brink of suicide. We often blamed others for the results of our actions; that was our way of dealing with guilt and shame and of avoiding personal responsibility. Our avoidance behavior only resulted in another brick being placed in our wall of denial.

Finally, we faced reality. We accepted personal responsibility for our actions, and we accepted the negative consequences of our actions; then we were able to make a *conscious* decision to stop our harmful behavior.

To get the most from this principle, we had to add two more parts. Some of us had been severely hurt by others in the past. Some of us suffered from debilitating emotional effects of childhood trauma. But we could not move forward until we became *willing* to forgive those who harmed us. Also, we found we had to be *willing* to forgive ourselves. The act of forgiving ourselves was often much harder than forgiving others.

Principle 3

We learned we are never justified in using violent words, threats,
or actions to feel powerful over people, situations, or things.

Finally we understood why we used anger, violence, and rage. Finally we understood why we repeated the same old pattern, even when we hated ourselves for our actions. Now we could move forward to a solution to the problem.

Finally we accepted the idea that violence was never justified, *except in cases where our own lives or the lives of our loved ones were at risk.* Having accepted that idea, we could move toward developing new ideas about the meaning of anger and to search for and find nonviolent ways to feel empowered.

Principle 4

We found new ways to feel personal power that
do not violate other people's right to feel safe.

This principle helped speed up our progress. We worked hard to learn new skills. What we learned led to feelings of personal power and influence that we could feel proud of instead of ashamed of. Some of us learned a more satisfying way to earn a living. Some of us went into business for ourselves. Some of us returned to school to learn a new trade or career. Some of us became professional counselors or therapists.

Principle 5

We are committed to treating all people and their property with
the dignity and respect that we, ourselves, deserve and expect.

It was hard for some of us to put this principle into practice. Some of us had been hurt badly. We often wished to retaliate, yet we decided we could no longer hold grudges. We knew we had to move forward, and we knew we had to let go of the pain of the past in order to do so.

Principle 6

We discovered that negative beliefs fueled our anger.
We have adopted new, empowering beliefs to take their place.

We discovered that some of our beliefs kept us stuck; the ones that kept us stuck were negative beliefs. They limited us. We found we could discard those beliefs and could learn new beliefs—new beliefs that would help us change our angry behavior and keep it changed.

Principle 7

We believe we can change. And we believe we have a purpose beyond the gratification of our own personal desires.

Many of us felt we were beyond help. We felt hopeless and helpless. We believed we could not change our violent behavior and were doomed to continue hurting those we loved and to continue suffering further personal losses. We were greatly relieved when we found that we *could* change. The most empowering thing we learned was that we had a *purpose*. We learned that our mission could help us to grow in an astonishing way.

Principle 8

We are being transformed by working this program. Now we forgive those who harmed us and we forgive ourselves. Now we choose to continue our path of emotional, mental, and spiritual growth, and to help others find their pathway to peace.

We practiced the Pathways to Peace Principles. We went to Pathways to Peace meetings. We learned from each other. Then we discovered our lives had been transformed.

But we did not stop there. We continued to practice the Principles; we stayed on the path; we kept growing and changing.

We were transformed. We felt obligated, even compelled, to help others who were driven by anger, rage, and violence.

The eighth is the only one of the Pathways to Peace Principles that refers to *spirituality*. We believe that a change of character must take place. Therefore, we needed to pay attention to the spiritual part of our whole self. Pathways to Peace is not a religious program, but we recognize that all human beings need some form of spiritual food, and in that sense, Pathways to Peace is spiritual. However, we find it best to leave it up to each individual Pathways to Peace member to choose his or her own spiritual food. We want to be happily free of anger and rage, so we must follow a balanced path of change and growth at all vital levels of human functioning. Spirituality is one of the vital levels.

Of all the Pathways to Peace Principles, the eighth has the most power. But you cannot fully take advantage of the eighth principle and effectively apply it to your life unless you also apply the other seven.

The eighth principle talks about transformation. *Transformation* means big change. When you *transform*, you change in a big way. You change your *character*. You change and grow at every part of your whole self. But transformation is a lifelong process, not a single event. Transformation requires lifelong commitment and lifelong growth in all eight parts of your whole self. Transformation is a journey.

The journey won't always be easy; things will get tough from time to time. Don't get discouraged, and never, never, never give up.

❧ The Pathways to Peace Rules ❧

Here are the Pathways to Peace rules. The rules assure the safety of Pathways to Peace members.

1. We agree not to share information outside the group.

2. We agree not to be violent at meetings.

3. We agree not to attend meetings under the influence of alcohol or other drugs.

4. We agree not to bring weapons to the group.

❧ The Pathways to Peace Mentor Program ❧

Pathways to Peace has a mentor program. A "mentor" is a *wise teacher* or *trusted advisor*. A mentor is sometimes called a "role model." A role model is someone who sets an example. A role model can set good examples or bad examples. A Pathways to Peace mentor is expected to set a good example.

The Pathways to Peace mentor program strengthens the power of the group. Pathways to Peace mentors help out new members. They are not counselors. They charge no fees.

A Message from Bill

The first Pathways to Peace group was formed in January 1998 in Jamestown, New York. By the end of the year there were many others. A group started in Dunkirk, New York. A month later a Pathways to Peace group began in Ripley, New York, near the Pennsylvania border. Then Pathways to Peace went to Buffalo, as well as Albany, New York. Around this time, a counselor at a mental health center in Tucson, Arizona, bought *The Pathways to Peace Anger Management Workbook* and started a group there. A group opened in Sierra Vista, Arizona, soon after. Then Pathways to Peace appeared on the scene in Knoxville, Tennessee, and Cleveland, Ohio. What started out as a single group to help half a dozen people has become a movement. Existing groups are growing in size. Recently, Pathways to Peace went north of the border. A group has formed in St. Catharines, Ontario, Canada. We have even received requests for information about our program from as far away as England, New Zealand, and Australia. Our website has been visited by people from every continent.

Appendix 2

How You Can Start a Pathways to Peace Group in Your Area

You have completed *The Pathways to Peace Anger Management Workbook.* Now you will want to reinforce what you have learned for yourself and share what you have learned with others. The best way to do this is to participate in a Pathways to Peace group in your area. If there are no groups in your area, you will want to start one.

◆ Find a Place to Meet

Starting a group is not difficult. First you need a place to meet. Contact the pastors of some churches in your area. Ask them if they would donate space. Human services agencies that do anger management counseling might help you find space.

◆ Get the Word Out

Next you will need to get the word out. Contact your local newspaper. Ask them to put an announcement in their calendar of events; there is usually no charge. Shoppers guides will usually place an announcement for you at no charge. In the announcement, simply say a Pathways to Peace group is forming. Mention that the group is free. Make sure the location, along with the day and time of the meeting, is included. Include your phone number in the announcement and ask people to call for details.

Also contact radio stations and cable TV stations. They often offer free public announcement services. Another good way to get the word out is to place flyers on super-market bulletin boards. Get permission from the store manager to post some flyers. Twelve-step groups, such as Alcoholics Anonymous (AA) or Narcotics Anonymous (NA), would probably post some of your flyers at their meetings. You could even ask to start a Pathways to Peace group at the local jail. County probation offices are also good resources.

◆ Refreshments

You may want to provide free coffee at the meeting. If so, pass the basket for a small donation (one dollar or less) to help with costs.

⚈ Meeting Times ⚈

Evenings from 7:00 to 8:00 P.M. are usually the best meeting times for most people. It is difficult to get people to commit to a Pathways to Peace meeting on weekends, or during daytime hours during the regular work week.

It will take time and effort to get a Pathways to Peace group up and running in your area, and it may take a small amount of money. But the result will be more than worthwhile. You will have an opportunity to help yourself. You will have an opportunity to help other people—people like yourself; people who want to stop verbally or physically abusing family members; people who want to stop abusing friends, employers, pets, or even themselves; people who are stuck because they don't know where to turn. You can help. You have a new understanding of the nature of anger and rage. You have new skills. You can help provide a place for others to turn.

⚈ Pathways to Peace Materials ⚈

In order to start a Pathways to Peace group, you will need a few materials. You will need at least one copy of *The Pathways to Peace Anger Management Workbook*. You may order workbooks from Hunter House.

On pages 207–209 of this workbook, you will find the Pathways to Peace Meeting Facilitator's Guide. When you start your group, use the guide to assure a successful meeting. Simply keep it in front of you and read from it.

On pages 210–212 of this workbook you will find large print versions of Eight Principles of Pathways to Peace, Pathways to Peace Rules, and Pathways to Peace Definition of Violence. As you will discover when you read the Facilitator's Guide, these three pages should be read at the opening of every Pathways group meeting. You may make copies of these three pages for this purpose. You may want to have these pages laminated in plastic to keep them in good condition.

However, you are asked not to copy any other parts of the workbook. *The Pathways to Peace Anger Management Workbook* is copyrighted material. Each group member should purchase his or her own workbook. When a member cannot afford to purchase a workbook, the group should use money from "the basket" to purchase a workbook for the member. Pathways to Peace groups may also purchase workbooks at the wholesale price, if a minimum of five workbooks are purchased at one time. Call Pathways to Peace for details (see page 209).

Pathways to Peace Group Structure Guidelines

Each Pathways to Peace group is composed of a volunteer primary facilitator, a volunteer secretary/treasurer, a volunteer assistant, and participants.

◆ **Primary Facilitator's Responsibilities**

■ locate meeting space

- get the word out (publicity)

- choose a "volunteer" as secretary/treasurer

- open and close the meeting

- set up meeting, assisted by volunteers

- keep the physical space in proper order

- pass the basket for donations at end of meeting

- communicate with Pathways to Peace main office

- serve one to three months as facilitator

- obtain and "train" alternative facilitators

◆ Secretary/Treasurer's Responsibilities

- record donations collected at meetings and from book sales

- maintain group treasury (bank account or just an envelope)

- purchase workbooks from Pathways to Peace main office

- make workbooks available for purchase by members

- provide indigent members with "free" workbooks using donations collected from group basket donations and "profits" from book sales

- present brief financial report to group once per month

- send small quarterly donation from group treasury to PTP main office. May act as co-facilitator at request of primary facilitator

- may act as facilitator when primary facilitator is absent

◆ Volunteer Assistant's Responsibilities

- help facilitator set up meeting

- make the coffee

- request funds for coffee from secretary/treasurer

- may act as facilitator when primary facilitator and secretary/treasurer are both absent

◆ Participants' Responsibilities

- be on time

- comply with group rules

◆ Introduction

The *Pathways to Peace* workbook is the official guidebook for all Pathways to Peace programs. The workbook should be used as the primary educational tool for the groups. Pathways to Peace group participants need to learn about the content of the workbook in order to help themselves and each other change their behavior and grow toward their higher selves.

At least some time should be spent reading from the workbook during each group session. Ideally, twenty to thirty minutes should be devoted to reading the workbook during the first half hour of the group. Groups should cycle through one reading of the entire workbook every four to eight months. Reading of the material should be voluntary. If a participant does not wish to read, they may simply say "I pass" or "I would rather not read today." No one should feel they are being forced to read.

After reading from the workbook during the first half of the group session, the last half should be opened up for comments from the participants. The facilitator should help the group members focus their comments on the content of the workbook. Once the reading from the workbook has been completed, participants should also be encouraged to talk in a general way about personal issues that pertain to anger and rage. When discussion veers from the main purpose of the Pathways to Peace program and message, the facilitator should use the Pathways to Peace Eight Principles, Rules, and Definition of Violence to help the group refocus.

Using the workbook and the materials as the primary focus of the meetings will keep the group process from breaking down into "blame and complain" sessions.

◆ Meeting Format

Meetings last approximately one hour. The steps to facilitating a Pathways to Peace meeting are listed below.

1. Open meeting. Start by introducing yourself to the group.

    "Hi everybody. My name is _____, and I have a problem with my anger."

    Then starting on your right or left, go around the group and have everyone else introduce themselves by first name and tell why they are at the meeting.

2. Guide members through a brief relaxation exercise to help them reduce their stress level. Take about thirty seconds. Speak slowly, using a soft tone.

    "Take a deep breath in, then a deep breath out and relax your posture. Continuing to breathe in a relaxed way, slowly and deeply, reflect on how important it is to learn how to relax in this way. Practice this skill several times a day, until it becomes a part of you. Use this technique whenever you feel stressed or whenever you feel an anger trigger of any kind."

3. Ask a member to read the Pathways to Peace Principles.

4. Ask a member to read the Pathways to Peace Rules.

5. Ask a member to read the Pathways to Peace Definition of Violence.

6. Ask a member to read paragraph four on page 2, "Pathways to Peace: A Solution."

7. Make any announcements that would be of interest to the group.

8. Go directly to whatever workbook chapter the group is studying. Go around the room, starting on your left or right, and ask for volunteers to read a page or two from the chapter. Do not stop to do the workbook exercises with the entire group, unless the group has decided to do so. Ask the participants to complete the written work on their own time, before the group meets again. Continue reading until at least half of the chapter has been completed. Then ask members if they have any questions about the materials just read. If so, encourage members to help each other find the appropriate answers. Refer to the workbook, or to the Principles, Rules, or Definition of Violence, when confusion occurs.

9. Ask members if any problems or issues having to do with anger have come up over the past week about which they would like some feedback from the group. Start on your right or left, and give each person a chance to comment. Participants who do not wish to comment may simply say, "I pass" or "I don't want to comment tonight." Those who wish to comment should be allowed two to five minutes to speak. Then go to the next person. Do not allow a few individuals to take up most of the time. Participants may comment more than once if everyone else has been given an opportunity to comment.

10. Approximately two minutes before ending the meeting, pass the basket for rent and coffee donations. (This is voluntary. No one should be made to feel they have to donate, and no one should put more than a dollar or two into the basket.)

11. Close the meeting with the following meditation:

"Everyone sit back and get into a more relaxed posture again. Take a slow, deep breath. Maintaining that more relaxed posture, continue to breathe slowly and deeply. Be aware for a moment or two of all the angry people all over the world, and of what they have lost because of their anger and rage. Some of them have lost their families; some have lost their jobs; some have lost their freedom or their self-respect. Some have even lost their lives.

Be aware also of all of the victims of other people's anger and rage, and recognize they don't deserve the pain they are going through.

Be aware that it doesn't have to be that way for us anymore. We can meet together as we have today, and we can help each other find new ways to deal with the same old triggers—new ways that do not violate another person's right to feel safe.

Above all, recognize that everybody in this room deserves to be happy, as long as it is not at someone else's expense. Have a good week, everybody. See you next week."

Before leaving the meeting site, make sure everything is in order (lights off, water taps off, etc.).

If You Need Assistance

If you need help starting or facilitating a group, call Pathways to Peace. We will be glad to do what we can to assist you.

Pathways to Peace
PO Box 259
Cassadaga NY 14718
(800) 775-4212
E-mail: transfrm@netsync.net
Website: www.pathwaystopeaceinc.com

∼ *The Pathways to Peace Principles* ∼

Principle 1

We admitted we have a problem with anger and have harmed people, property, and ourselves. Whenever possible, we make amends or restitution.

Principle 2

We accepted responsibility for our actions and decided to stop our harmful behavior. We became willing to forgive those who harmed us, and to forgive ourselves for the harm we caused others.

Principle 3

We learned we are never justified in using violent words, threats, or actions to feel powerful over people, situations, or things.

Principle 4

We found new ways to feel personal power that do not violate other people's right to feel safe.

Principle 5

We are committed to treating all people and their property with the dignity and respect that we, ourselves, deserve and expect.

Principle 6

We discovered that negative beliefs fueled our anger. We have adopted new, empowering beliefs to take their place.

Principle 7

We believe we can change. And we believe we have a purpose beyond the gratification of our own personal desires.

Principle 8

We are being transformed by working this program. Now we forgive those who harmed us and forgive ourselves. Now we choose to continue our path of emotional, mental, and spiritual growth, and to help others find their pathway to peace.

~ *The Pathways to Peace Rules* ~

Pathways to Peace has a few rules to protect the identity and safety of those who participate in the Pathways to Peace program. The rules are as follows:

1. We agree not to share information outside the group.

2. We agree not to be violent at meetings.

3. We agree not to attend meetings under the influence of alcohol or other drugs.

4. We agree not to bring weapons into the group.

~ The Pathways to Peace ~
Definition of Violence

What Is Violence?

V I O L E N C E

◀ *Verbal Abuse ~ Violent Threats/Postures ~ Physical Violence* ▶

Imagine a line stretching from wall to wall across a room.

The left-hand wall represents verbal abuse: name-calling,
screaming and yelling, and sarcasm.

Verbal threats or threatening postures belong
somewhere near the center of the line.

The right-hand wall represents physical violence
that may result in injury or death.

It is all violence.

© 2003, Pathways to Peace, Inc.

The Pathways to Peace

Anger Management Workbook

The Pathways to Peace Anger Management Workbook

The Pathways to Peace Anger Management Workbook is available from Hunter House. Teen and Spanish-language versions will also become available. To order, see the last page.

The Niagara Falls Metaphor Video

The video graphically compares anger and rage to a trip down the Niagara River and over the Falls, as described in Chapter 6 of the workbook. It is a great tool, especially for groups, to help understand the anger process.

Laminated Copies of the Pathways to Peace Principles, Rules, and Definition of Violence

Made to last, these laminated copies are for use by Pathways to Peace support groups.

Pathways to Peace Program Master Package

This package is a cost-effective way to make the Pathways to Peace program available to schools, institutions, organizations, or agencies. It includes *The Pathways to Peace Anger Management Workbook* in a loose-leaf binder; the Niagara Falls metaphor video; and laminated copies of the Principles, Rules, and Definition of Violence.

On-Site Introductory Seminars Also Available

Pathways to Peace can come to you and introduce the Pathways to Peace program to your community or organization.

For prices, more information, or to order, contact:

Pathways to Peace • PO Box 259 • Cassadaga NY 14718 • (800) 775-4212
E-mail: transfrm@netsync.net • Website: www.pathwaystopeaceinc.com

Making the Peace: *A 15-Session Violence Prevention Curriculum for Young People*

by Paul Kivel and Allan Creighton, with the Oakland Men's Project

This is a highly respected violence prevention curriculum for youth-group leaders and educators. The ready-to-use exercises, roleplays, and discussion guidelines show students how to explore the roots of violence in the community and their lives; deal with dating violence, fights, suicide, guns, and sexual harassment; and develop practical techniques for stopping violence. The Oakland Men's Project, an affiliate of Todos, is a nonprofit organization dedicated to violence prevention and to building alliances across gender, race, sexual orientation, and age.

192 PAGES | 15 PHOTOS | 35 HANDOUTS | PAPERBACK $29.95

Days of Respect: *Organizing a School-Wide Violence Prevention Program*

by Ralph Cantor, with Paul Kivel, Allan Creighton, and the Oakland Men's Project

This is a step-by-step guide for designing and staging a collaborative, schoolwide event that brings young people, teachers, parents, and the community together to create respect and tolerance in their school. The program, developed by an experienced teacher and the Oakland Men's Project, emphasizes hands-on practice in building nonviolent relationships and includes planning outlines and checklists, timetables, permission slips, training exercises on gender and race, and evaluations.

64 PAGES | 6 PHOTOS | 21 HANDOUTS | PAPERBACK $17.95

Making Allies, Making Friends: *A Curriculum for Making the Peace in Middle School*

by Hugh Vasquez, M. Nell Myhand, and Allan Creighton, with Todos

This new curriculum for students in grades 6 through 9 integrates with the Making the Peace program but also stands on its own. More than 30 innovative classroom sessions address diversity and violence issues that middle-schoolers face. Some of the themes are: What respect is, Who am I / Who are my people?, Safety, and more. This timely and carefully crafted work will be a valuable resource for middle-school personnel and teachers of violence prevention, youth development, conflict resolution, social studies, art, and theater.

224 PAGES | 11 PHOTOS | 37 HANDOUTS | PAPERBACK $29.95

Helping Teens Stop Violence: *A Practical Guide for Counselors, Educators, and Parents*

by Allan Creighton with Paul Kivel

Today's teenagers may be subjected to violence at home, at school, and in society. For several years, the Oakland Men's Project (OMP) and Battered Women's Alternatives (BWA) conducted seminars and workshops with teens and adults around the country, weaving issues of gender, race, age, and sexual orientation into frank discussions about male violence and its roots. This book by founders of the OMP and BWA provides guidelines on how to help teenagers help themselves out of the cycle of abuse and find ways to deal with and reduce the violence in the world around them.

168 PAGES | 16 PHOTOS | PAPERBACK $19.95

Keeping Kids Safe: *A Child Sexual Abuse Prevention Manual*

by Pnina Tobin, MPA, and Sue Levinson Kessner, M.S.

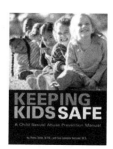

The threat of sexual abuse is constant, and it is crucial to teach children how to recognize when they are in danger of being abused by strangers or people they know and how to obtain help. *Keeping Kids Safe* contains curricula for ages 3–7 and 8–11 with word-for-word scripts and workshops. Children are taught to distinguish between wanted and unwanted touch, and to say "No!" and get help. A Facilitator's Guide informs educators about myths and facts about child sexual abuse, development issues and indicators of abuse, and reporting procedures and follow-up methods.

160 PAGES | 31 PHOTOGRAPHS | PAPERBACK $34.95 | SPIRALBOUND $39.95 | REVISED 2ND EDITION

More Resources for Adults and Families

When Violence Begins at Home:
A Comprehensive Guide to Understanding and Ending Domestic Abuse... by K. J. Wilson, Ed.D.

Written by a survivor of domestic violence, the first edition of this highly recommended and far-reaching reference provided professionals and victims of abuse with guidance on everything from indicators of an abusive relationship to domestic violence legislation, and from antiburnout tips for helpers to advice on leaving an abusive partner. This updated edition addresses new research and programs; information on date rape drugs, cyber-stalking, pregnancy and domestic violence; and more. Current controversial social and legal issues are covered, and two new chapters devote attention to domestic violence in the military and to the challenging role of those who work with battered women and their children.

480 PAGES | 7 ILLUS. | PAPERBACK $29.95 | REVISED 2ND EDITION

Counseling Victims of Violence: *A Handbook for Helping Professionals*
by Sandra L. Brown, M.A.

Each chapter of *Counseling Victims of Violence* offers practical guidance on a specific type of violence victimization, what issues must be addressed during crisis intervention, secondary victimizations, and social services resources needed. A special feature is the quick-glance reference charts that outline the basics and summarize each chapter's contents.

304 PAGES | 3 ILLUS. | PAPERBACK $24.95 | REVISED 2ND EDITION

Peace in Everyday Relationships
Resolving Conflicts in Your Personal and Work Life

by Sheila Alson and Gayle Burnett, Ph.D.

As the world becomes—or feels—more and more unstable, we must seek harmony close to home. We need the best possible relationships with spouses, families, friends, coworkers, and bosses. In this practical guide, two successful conflict-resolution specialists outline how we can negotiate both the big conflicts and the smaller disagreements in our daily lives—with neither side feeling like a loser. A special chapter addresses how to deal with difficult people.

240 PAGES | 1 ILLUS. | PAPERBACK $14.95

Free Yourself from an Abusive Relationship: *Seven Steps to Taking Back Your Life*
by Andrea Lissette, M.A., CDVC, and Richard Kraus, Ph.D.

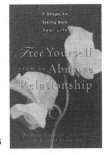

A lifesaving guide for women who are victims of violence and abuse. Step One describes different kinds of abuse. Step Two is about abusers and who they abuse, with sections on children and senior citizens. Step Three deals with crises, stalking, rape, and assault. It includes an in-depth look at legal help and court proceedings. Step Four shows women how to live as survivors, with practical advice on money matters and work issues. Step Five discusses the decision to stay or leave, and Steps Six and Seven move from healing and rebuilding to becoming and remaining abuse-free.

304 PAGES | 2 ILLUS. | PAPERBACK $17.95

I Can Make My World a Safer Place: *A Kid's Book about Stopping Violence*
by Paul Kivel • Illustrations and games by Nancy Gorrell

This book for children ages 6–11 shows what they can do to find alternatives to violence in their lives. Kivel explains public danger (gangs, fights, and drug-related violence) and private danger (sexual assault and domestic violence) and gives suggestions for staying safe. Simple text and activities such as mazes and word searches encourage young readers to think about and promote peace. Activism is discussed, using examples such as César Chavez and Julia Butterfly. The multicultural drawings by Nancy Gorrell are playful and engaging, guiding the reader, reinforcing the text, and making difficult ideas easier to understand.

96 PAGES | 90 ILLUS. | PAPERBACK $14.95

To order or for our FREE catalog of books please see last page or call 1-800-266-5592

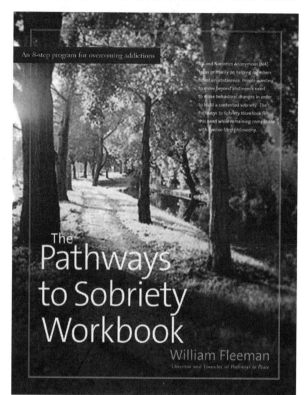